the luxury bathroom

the luxury bathroom

extraordinary spaces from the simple to the extravagant

samantha nestor

with jen renzi
photographs by
andrew french

Clarkson Potter/Publishers
New York

Copyright © 2008 by Samantha Nestor

Published in the United States by Clarkson Potter/Publishers, an
imprint of the Crown Publishing Group, a division of Random House,
Inc., New York.
www.crownpublishing.com
www.clarksonpotter.com

Clarkson N. Potter is a trademark and Potter and colophon are
registered trademarks of Random House, Inc.

Library of Congress Cataloging-in-Publication Data
Nestor, Samantha.
   The luxury bathroom : extraordinary spaces from the simple to the
extravagant / Samantha Nestor ; with Jen Renzi ; photographs by
Andrew French.
   Includes index.
   1. Bathrooms.   2. Interior decoration.   I. Renzi, Jen.
II. French, Andrew (Andrew Frederick), 1956–   III. Title.
   NK2117   B33N47   2008
   747.7'8—dc22   2008006767

ISBN 978-0-307-39370-8

Printed in China

Design by Richard Ferretti
Photographs by Andrew French

10   9   8   7   6   5   4   3   2   1

First Edition

for finn

contents

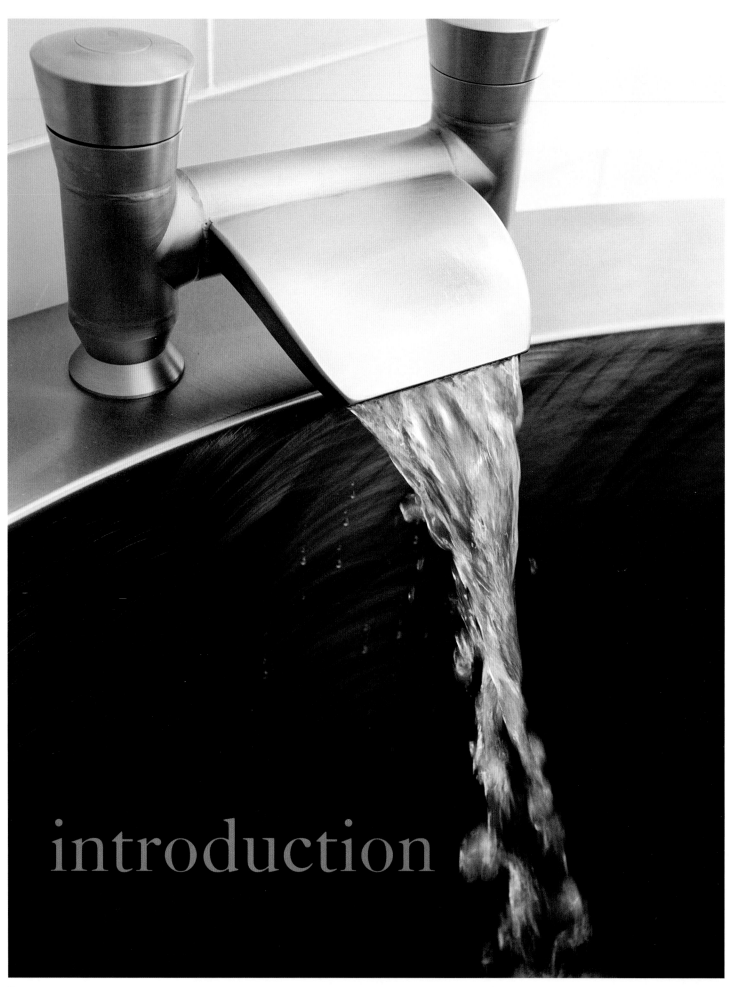

introduction

IN *THE HOUSE IN GOOD TASTE,* GRANDE DAME of design Elsie de Wolfe wrote, "The straightaway bathroom that one finds in apartments and small houses is difficult to make beautiful, but may be made airy and clean-looking, which is more important."

If de Wolfe were alive, I think she would be among the first to recognize that the phenomenal array of unique materials, the lavish budgets, and the limitless imagination of designers and builders have made bathrooms the new design frontier. Bathroom design has come a long way since her heyday in the early twentieth century, and to say that bathrooms now are at once beautiful, airy, and fresh is an understatement. The latest bathrooms don't just exemplify luxury but also redefine it, whether it is the luxury of providing relaxation or through the use of expensive, rare materials. Bathrooms are now essential elements in any fabulous home. The space has become a nucleus of style and taste, but perhaps it is most precious for seducing its owners to spend *time* there. And, after all, what is more luxurious than time?

What struck me when I first set out to develop *The Luxury Bathroom* is that trends are not guided by a popular architectural style; rather, interior design today is geared to our *personal* style—which is dictated by our way of life. Some bathrooms are locations for family gatherings; others represent the only respite from a hectic lifestyle. In the last decade, bedrooms were rewired to house an array of technology that invited lounging; kitchens expanded to assume the role of family room, with outrageous square footage and open floor plans; and living rooms became media rooms. But in the bathroom we stayed true to our Puritanical roots, boxing it in and imagining it as little more than a private closet with running water. Recently, however, we've stopped looking at this room as a one-note space. Sure, it still needs to fulfill a utilitarian purpose. But it's also the Cinderella star of a fancy dress ball.

Societal shifts have facilitated this sea change. Granted, designers' imaginations have soared with their clients' incomes and a plethora of decorative choices, but they are not dreaming in a vacuum. As Americans spend more time nesting and live more casually, they are redefining the way they use their homes. Some people want a private haven within their home. Others yearn for a spa experience. Many are inspired by the free flow of water, and see the bathroom as an opportunity to bring nature inside, or to make the inside feel like the outdoors. Perhaps most interesting, as the boundaries between public and private spaces in the home blur, the bathroom is becoming a playful, even trafficked, area. Sometimes it's a canvas for entertaining; at other times it teases with a grown-up, erotic game of peekaboo. Quite often its airiness, gadgets, and novelty draw in the whole clan and it becomes the new de facto family room. Ironically, that once boxed-in room is now the most versatile and exciting room in the house. Social taboos have been lifted and the bathroom has been freed to be the multiuse space of the home owner's dreams.

The Luxury Bathroom explores twenty-eight innovative baths. My criteria for luxury went beyond gold-plated faucets. More than anything, I was looking for surprises: in materials, in how the space—big or small—was designed, and in how the bathroom was used. I found them all over the place—Miami; Chicago; Los Angeles; Litchfield County, Connecticut. Nearly every bathroom has the same immovable features that exist for purely functional uses. But the way in which these items can be leveraged beyond their original intent and can disappear with the right magic from a clever architect or designer makes them unique. A sink can double as a wet bar; the vanity can hold a computer; a tub is just as much fun as a swimming pool.

Early in the process, my collaborator on the book, Jen Renzi, sent me a photograph of Miles Redd in his own bathroom noting that he held candlelit dinner parties there. I thought it was an anomaly. Then I learned about Jason Oliver Nixon and John Loecke's bath on the top floor of their Brooklyn brownstone. It affords ample room and opportunities to entertain by opening onto a fabulous deck. I realized that a trend was afoot. I was shocked and a little uncomfortable at first to think of using the bathroom to entertain. But once I saw the spaces, the new uses people found for their bathrooms made perfect sense. When you read about Redd's obsession with collecting and creating this mirrored room, you will see that the space couldn't be saved for his eyes only. And he even admits, "There's nothing like being in a mirrored room filled with candlelight. And, after a few glasses of wine, you don't even notice it's a bathroom." Loecke acknowledges, "The best view in the house is from this terrace—we look out onto sunny gardens and faraway Brooklyn apartments. It would have been a shame to make this space off-limits during parties."

Inviting people into the bathroom isn't just about welcoming guests. People are also creating spaces that can be described only as "family rooms": bathrooms that invite lingering and play. Benjamin Noriega-Ortiz explains, "Parents treat their kids differently these days. Maybe because they tend to be a little older when they start having babies, they like to be with their kids every second they can." This applies even in the bathroom, where tub time becomes quality bonding time. Children adore this room because it's often the space in which they have their parents all to themselves.

While entertaining and family baths have redefined private space by inviting people in, there is another kind of communal space that is more daring and even a bit naughty: I call it the voyeur space. Instead of receiving an invitation to enter, "guests" in the voyeur bathroom are more oglers at the velvet rope. The open, borderless space beckons to the outside world via see-through glass, soaking tubs plopped in the middle of a room, and wall-less showers that are essentially wet zones. Some people eliminate walls to create more space. Others want to commune with nature and seize spectacular outside views—even if it means knocking out a wall and replacing it with glass. In "Peekaboo, I See You," architect Alison Spear trades her client's privacy for breathtaking views of a boat-filled waterway in Miami. One person's exhibitionism is another person's need to feel as though he is outside.

The more classic bathrooms—the boudoir, the small bath, and the getaway spa—are being reinvented, too. The old boudoirs, for example, were nestled between the bedroom and the lady's dressing room, serving as a buffer zone between them. Modern boudoirs are extravagant sanctuaries where women can revel in hidden technologies, luxurious materials, and privacy. They are to recharge a woman and to give her the private space to transform. It is truly a place to let down one's hair. The boudoirs featured in *The Luxury Bathroom* are clever examples of how the owner's priorities informed design decisions. I love Celerie Kemble's bathroom that features a gorgeous armoire stocked with couture. Tile magnate Nancy Epstein's bath is about light, reflection, extraordinary materials, and unusual surfaces. The classic elements of a boudoir are all here, but, unlimited by convention, she's made it her own by using exotic elements like shagreen and Blacklip shell and reinterpreting design features she discovered in luxury hotels, historic architecture, and even fashion boutiques.

As a New Yorker, I knew that I would do a chapter on small spaces. Small spaces, such as the powder room, are a paean to creativity, thanks to the availability of new materials and a willingness to take design risks. One of my first jobs in New York was fund-raising for a museum. A prominent socialite was hosting a tea benefit in a magnificent Park Avenue apartment and I went to use the loo. I was mesmerized by the unique materials, especially on the walls. I know now that they were upholstered with horsehair fabric. I never forgot the impact that this tiny space had on me. That bath has since been renovated, but our featured project by Workshop/APD ("Hide and Seek," page 59) with its leather tile walls is my homage to the walls of a powder room that my twenty-three-year-old hands couldn't stop touching. Small bathrooms come in all shapes and styles, but they have one thing in common: they are showpieces of design possibilities.

I also knew that I couldn't write a book on luxury bathrooms without featuring home spas—there is nothing more à la mode than spas right now. Today "All work and no play . . ." means all work and no rest. Getting away from the world, relaxing and being pampered is a luxury. The trick was not to repeat the same products but to show different-looking retreats without simply making them look like a homogeneous hotel spa. From the desert to the beach to the Hollywood Hills and New York City, the spas featured here provide sanctuary to their owners with varied solutions.

The Luxury Bathroom journeys from the East and West Coasts to the Midwest, South, and Southwest, and features bathrooms in cities, in suburbs, and out in the country. Since there are so many choices and very few limitations, each chapter includes traditional, contemporary, and hybrid designs; together they function as a guide to help you identify the style of bath that will work best for you. Designers today are more clever than ever and their clients are open-minded and excited about the endless possibilities for this room. And so *The Luxury Bathroom* is a celebration not just of the bathroom but really of the imagination. It will inform and entertain as it cheers innovative bathroom design and the people who reside in these wonderful spaces. Ultimately, I hope the spaces and characters will inspire you to create your own personal perfect luxury bath.

escapes

Some people visit a Caribbean beach and relax to the lapping surf. Others jet off to a safari adventure. But for relaxation a little closer to home, many simply retreat to the most secluded spot in the house: their bathroom.

Stressed-out home owners are designing their full-time lodgings as places of sanctuary and centering. If work and life are increasingly incorporated into the home, why can't vacation time make an appearance there, too?

Taking cues from high-end hotels, designers are appointing baths with spalike indulgences: steam rooms, waterfall showerheads, and oversize soaking tubs equipped with light-therapy technologies. Some look even farther afield to other cultures for inspiration. Designer Jeff Andrews created a Zen retreat for a Los Angeles set decorator who spends her downtime unwinding in Japanese monasteries. The tranquil stone-clad bathroom balances monastic quietude with modern luxury, while supporting the elaborate Buddhist bathing rituals the owner has embraced abroad. This way, she can bring her travels home with her.

People often escape by communing with nature—even if that's just a matter of accessing nearby surroundings. After being stuck inside an office all day, who doesn't yearn for a little outdoor time? D. Crosby Ross's bathing oasis for a TV producer in Palm Springs is suited to restorative contemplation by harnessing the local elements. The master bathroom's back wall opens up fully to the yard so the client enjoys the sense of bathing outside—which he can also do, thanks to a palm tree out back that's been converted into a shower. Soaking under the stars is, to many, the ultimate means of escape—and the lucky can go to great lengths to achieve either the reality or the illusion.

Sometimes home owners seek refuge from—rather than embrace—the local context, particularly if they live in an extremely hot or cold environment. One example is René González's restful design for a Key Biscayne penthouse. The architect converted a windowless master bathroom into a cool and stunning oasis. The blissed-out scheme

Previous pages: In this steam shower, designed by Jeff Andrews, the seat is made from a slab of honed granite long enough for reclining.
Opposite: This Palm Springs bath, designed by R. Crosby Smith, features a Japanese soaking tub and an iconic plastic Verner Panton S chair.

channels the nearby ocean via surfaces clad in watery statuary marble and provides a great escape from the harsh Florida sun and heat.

Tucked away in the private quarters of the home, a bath is the perfect spot to indulge in a stylistic departure. For a New York businessman, decorator Scott Salvator crafted a nautical, wood-paneled bathroom reminiscent of a luxury yacht. The space is the only room in the penthouse tailored to his particular tastes, with a design that centers on a few simple but luxe materials.

Tired of shuttling back and forth between two homes at the end of a busy workweek, many combine their primary and weekend residences into one. It makes perfect sense: why further complicate one's already harried life, to say nothing of undertaking a two-hour drive on Friday and Sunday nights? Michaela Scherrer's Malibu client, for instance, has a master bath that mimics a high-end day spa, with a soothing palette of white plaster and teak that puts the emphasis on the lush surroundings it overlooks.

bathing au naturel

DAVID HALBREICH'S HOUSE IS JUST A FOUR-MINUTE DRIVE from the sun-kissed Malibu shores. But the vibe of the place is more tree house than beach cottage, with large picture windows overlooking tall stalks of bamboo, leafy junipers, and the mountains beyond. "It's an amazing location," he says. "I'm surrounded by nature and wildlife. In the mornings, I hear owls and choruses of birds." The soothing setting was the main draw for this busy corporate lawyer and father of three. Here, he has the best of both worlds: a secluded hideaway with the feel of a weekend retreat that's still an easy commute to his Los Angeles office. "Living in this house, I never feel the need to get away from it all," he explains.

While the location could not be beat, the architecture was a bit schizophrenic when he purchased the property. "It was built in 1989 and the bones were quite contemporary. But subsequent owners had kitsched them up with overwrought details. They didn't appreciate what a clean, simple design they had on their hands." So he hired interior designer Michaela Scherrer to pare things back: building a minimalist kitchen, removing tacked-on moldings from every window, and gutting an awkwardly laid out master bath. "It was a rabbit warren of rooms," says Halbreich. "There was a number of little closets and a winding hallway, which left only a narrow space for the bath. It was a tight squeeze in there—and it looked very seventies, with shiny white tiles." Says Scherrer, "From our first meeting, it was clear that David wanted a clean, relaxing space. The property is serene and peaceful, and the house— with all those moldings and icky tiles—didn't quite match."

Scherrer felt that the lush, almost forestlike surroundings should guide the design of the new master bath. She also hoped to strengthen the home's relationship with the elements: despite all the windows, the house had no porch. And while Halbreich had enclosed a side yard with a wall of bamboo and installed a patio and a Jacuzzi within, the plein air oasis was accessible only through a remote back door. So they opened up

Previous pages, left: A handheld showerhead is mounted low on the wall between the shower and the tub so it can be used from either location. Below a carved-teak stool, a slatted teak shower mat lies flush with the concrete-tile floor; the drain is hidden below. The oversize tub is sunk 5 inches below the floor to make the room feel more spacious. **Opposite:** For David Halbreich's master bathroom, designer Michaela Scherrer installed 24-inch square concrete floor tiles. The bathroom's serene color palette makes the space recede, drawing the eye out to the leafy yard. The French doors have a layer of removable translucent film, offering privacy until the bamboo outside grows high enough to block neighboring houses.

the exterior wall between the master bath and the adjacent patio and installed French doors and a large casement window. Halbreich will eventually build a short flight of stairs so he can step down from the bath to the Jacuzzi; for now, he can delight in the newly created view.

Within, Scherrer and Halbreich reworked the layout to make the room feel expansive. (Building an addition was not an option since the house had the maximum interior footage per city codes.) A short, straight hallway from the bedroom now leads past a small toilet room, a walk-in closet, and a wall of built-in teak cabinets before culminating in the main bathing area. Combining the closets and moving the toilet to the side created a more orderly procession of spaces, while sliding doors make the hallway more navigable. For visual continuity, the doors hang from teak fasciae, which match the cabinetry throughout the entire suite. "I wanted the doors themselves to be teak, but we had to use drywall due to budgetary constraints," says Scherrer. "The fascia was a good compromise."

Scherrer's design of the bathroom itself is a master class in serenity, with concrete floors, hand-troweled plaster walls, and teak accents. The white-on-white color palette and smooth flow from one material to the next lets the interior play second fiddle to the views. "The eye is always drawn to the farthest point of color—in this case, the greenery outside," Scherrer says. "It's a trick to make the space seem bigger."

One wall is given over to an 8-foot-long cast-concrete sink with a sloping basin that spills water to a hidden drain beneath. A plaster backsplash in the same hue and texture as the sink makes the vanity look like one continuous surface. "The sink was inspired by a photo David showed me when we initially met to discuss the project," says Scherrer. "It was one of the first elements we chose." Freestanding drawers below, which can be pulled out to access the sink's plumbing behind, are made of oil-finished linear-grain teak. Scherrer selected each piece of teak by hand, choosing a tight grain so the cabinets don't look too busy. Flanking the vanity are minimalist, dimmable light fixtures with custom stainless-steel back plates. "I prefer lighting to be functional rather than decorative. I like it to disappear."

Opposite, above: The 8-foot-long cast-concrete sink has a sloping basin with a hidden drain. Water spills down the angled surface into a near-invisible channel at the back. **Opposite, below:** The sink has two wall-mounted faucets. The plaster backsplash is the same hue and texture as the concrete sink, making it look like one continuous surface. Seen from below—the vantage point of the soaking tub—the super-shallow sink looks as if it's just a countertop, making the space seem less bathroomlike. Below the sink, a pair of teak cabinets can be pulled out to expose a hinged flap, which provides access to plumbing behind. A silvery leather ottoman provides a postsoak perch to enjoy the view.

An open shower defined by a teak floor mat creates openness. "A shower in the middle of a room is my favorite thing," says Scherrer. "People are often scared to do something so out of the ordinary, but David was game." The mat is recessed so it's flush with the floor: the continuous plane gives the room a much cleaner line. Beside the shower, the large casement window can be cracked open for a view of the patio.

To the right, an oversize soaking tub—filled by a ribbonlike floor-mounted fixture—is set 5 inches below the floor level. "Sinking it gave the whole space a more Zen flavor, making the lines from one element to another flow more harmoniously," says Scherrer. The low tub surround is also easier for Halbreich's children to hop over. "The bathroom was designed as my retreat, but I can't keep my kids out," he says. "Every time I turn around there's another kid in there. The tub is like an indoor pool to them." He can relate: "It is incredibly comfortable, and so nice to sit there with candles lit and look out at the greenery."

Hand-troweled plaster walls subtly set apart this wet zone from the rest of the space. "The shift in texture from plaster to paint is a way of creating separation without adding partitions," says Scherrer. The floor is surfaced in matching off-white concrete. Scherrer had wanted to install a poured slab-concrete floor, but there was not enough reinforcement below to support the weight. So she chose 24-inch square tiles to achieve the same look, sandblasted for a rugged finish. "It's a bright space," says Halbreich. "But because of all the subtle textures, it's quite cozy—especially at night with the lights dimmed, as you look out over the yard."

These textured white surfaces look precious, but Scherrer insists that they are low maintenance. "I have a concrete bathtub in my own home, and I never have a problem keeping it clean—even though I float flower petals in it." (Halbreich has a tall plaster planter at the foot of his tub for the same purpose.) Oil-based products, she says, are the only thing you have to watch out for. But a little aging is part of the charm; concrete, plaster, and teak are living, breathing elements. "You have to be open to letting materials patinate. There is so much beauty in nature," says Scherrer.

Opposite: Plaster walls define the wet areas—the shower, the tub, and the space around the vanity. Slim chrome shower accessories from Italy reinforce the clean-lined architecture. Recessed wall niches by the shower and the tub are big enough for large shampoo bottles.

yachtsman's haven

THE OWNERS of a grand New York triplex faced a classic conundrum. While the man of the house was happy to indulge his wife's aesthetic in the public areas, he favored something a bit more subdued—and, yes, manly—for his own domain.

Here, minimal and masculine translates to a cocoon of exotic millwork, treated to a lacquered finish that adds a hint of sheen. The effect is nautical, like the interior of a luxury yacht. Almost every square inch of the room is paneled in quarter-sawn African zebrawood—vertically, so it creates the illusion of more headroom. Designer Scott Salvator had the door leading into the bathroom from the dressing area faux-painted to match the boiserie.

Jerusalem limestone clads the floor and vanity as well as the glass-enclosed steam shower (placed in the middle of the room to take advantage of views out both windows). "Jerusalem limestone is very evenly colored," says Salvator.

The space feels more like a library than a bath, thanks largely to Salvator's choice of lighting. Above the toilet he installed a wall sconce. To light a built-in dressing table, he used a mercury-glass table lamp whose silvery sheen reflects the nickel accents detailing the shower stall and the floor-mounted towel bar.

Like the interior of a Gulfstream jet, the beautiful woodwork disguises practical details for this man on the move, including full-height closets that hide behind mirrored doors. A flip-up bench below the window—a perfect poststeam perch to take in the fifteenth-floor views—stores towels. But the best part about the design of this manly boudoir? His wife likes it, too.

Wall panels and cabinets are solid, quarter-sawn African zebrawood with a lacquer finish. Salvator chose the nickel hardware to complement the warm wood.

a modern approach
to zen style

KIKI GIET LIVES IN A MIDCENTURY MODERN HOME high up in the Hollywood Hills, with views that most people would envy (and that the rest would find perhaps too dizzying for their taste). Designed in 1959 by Fred Kreipl, a student of LA architect Richard Neutra, the earthy, low-slung house has a living room wrapped in glass walls and a dramatically cantilevered porch that levitates precariously over a steeply sloping cliff.

The architect was so fixated on views from the living areas that he neglected the inner sanctum—namely, a windowless corner of the master suite that housed both closet and bath. "I'd lie in bed and look into that dark space and think, I know that on the other side of that wall is the most beautiful view in the house," says Giet.

So she decided to bring this overlooked nook to its full potential and design a new master bathroom in the process. "Kiki had been renovating bit by bit. She had waited five long years before tackling this part of the house, so she wanted to build her dream bathroom," explains her designer, Jeff Andrews. Her list of priorities included as much square footage as possible (even if closet space had to be sacrificed), a soaking tub with a view, and a Zen-like design—with respect to both form and function.

When not working around the clock designing elaborate sets for TV commercials, Giet often retreats to a monastery in Japan, where she has embraced the culture's elaborate bathing rituals. "You set up little stools around a soaking tub and wash before you soak," she says. "The process involves lots of scrubbing. The idea is to cleanse and purify your soul." To support this water-intensive ritual, her bathroom needed to function as one big wet zone. So Andrews sketched out a design that would clad almost the entire space in stone.

They began demolition not knowing what they'd find once the walls came down, says Andrews. "It was one surprise after another"—most of them, thankfully,

Previous pages, left: The mosaic accent wall extends from the tub all the way into the shower. The patterning of the tiles, which are made of fragments of different stones, has an abstract, sticklike design inspired by bamboo stalks—which Giet also grows on her property. At the foot of the tub, Jeff Andrews designed a wall niche to hold bath accessories as well as Kiki Giet's devotional objects. A sculptural carved-wood chair holds towels nearby. Previous pages, right: Pottery designed by Adam Silverman is prominently displayed. Opposite: Andrews deployed four different but complementary styles of stone throughout the bathroom so that the surfaces have variety but don't look too busy.

good ones. The drop ceiling disguised a lovely network of wood beams, which the designer exposed. When they broke through the exterior walls to create a wraparound corner window, the view was indeed spectacular—an ideal spot for the soaking tub. The only issue they encountered was structural: this corner of the house cantilevers over the lower floors, and structural reinforcement was required to support the weight of all the stone. "My contractor calls every time we have an earthquake, but it's proven to be very solid," says Giet.

With the additional beams shoring up the foundation, Andrews was free to use as much stone as the budget would allow. He surfaced the back wall in a stunning mosaic featuring an abstracted bamboo motif, and elsewhere chose marble that's similar in color, but with mellower veining. "Because the mosaic has a lot of pattern, the other surfaces needed to be a bit quieter— but still have personality," says the designer. "So I picked four slightly varied textures. The difference is subtle, but you can notice it at various times of the day."

For the shower floor, they chose pebbly river rocks, which the tile contractor was patient enough to let Giet place by hand. "It was very meditative and a great way to commune with the space," she says. The contractor was also willing to indulge her obsession with the mitered corners used along the edges of her marble-tiled vanity. "I wanted them cut at *exactly* forty-five degrees," says Giet. "I hate looking at the thickness of tile."

The vanity's walnut cabinets were designed to match the built-ins in the adjacent master bedroom, which are original to the house. Andrews customized the configuration of the drawers to accommodate all of Giet's toiletries. "I'm a bottle queen," she says, "but I don't want to look at them all the time." Accordingly, says Andrews, "I put a lot of thought into the width and depth of particular drawers. Such a Zen aesthetic is restful, but not, typically, the easiest space to live in if you have lots of stuff."

To hammer out nuts-and-bolts details, Andrews asks clients probing questions that make them consider lifestyle patterns. "It's all the little things: Do you like to keep extra toilet paper out or hidden away? Do you

Opposite, clockwise from above left: The vintage chinoiserie-style pendant light is actually a table lamp reengineered to hang upside down. Rather than position the skylight flush with the shower's ceiling, Giet asked that it be extended above the roofline, like a chimney, and surfaced with stone. Control knobs for the shower are placed in the corner so they can be easily accessed from within but don't distract from the overall Zen-like effect of the space. Andrews chose a minimalist wall-hung toilet to make it easier to clean the floor below.

prefer your towels folded or hung? Do you like to hang them on a bar or a hook? Do you use bar soap or liquid cleanser? If these features become an afterthought, it's not good design."

This sort of thinking inspired Andrews's placement of the shower controls on the low partition wall *opposite* the showerhead, rather than right below it—reachable from just outside the shower door so Giet can adjust the temperature before hopping in. The steam-equipped shower also has a fully operable skylight. "I wanted a sense of illumination coming through, but didn't want to see the actual window from within the shower. I was inspired by the work of artist James Turrell, who creates these glowing boxes of light," she explains. Rather than install the skylight flush with the ceiling, Andrews designed it to extend 4 feet above the roofline, like a chimney lined in stone. A bench beneath is big enough for Giet to lie down on. Carved from a single slab of granite, the bench is smoothed over in a supple, honed finish. "It was tough convincing the stone guys to do the finish—they thought I was crazy," she says. "Honing takes out all the flecks and shine and makes it beautifully dull, which I love."

A carved-wood chair outside the shower is an artful pedestal for towels. The piece forms a sculptural accent in the calm stone space, tying together the Zen look of the room with the midcentury modern aesthetic of the rest of the house. A few feet away, Giet had a floor drain installed between the bathtub and the shower to accommodate splashing from her Zen bathing rituals.

One day, Giet hopes to add a *zendo* to her house—a meditation hall for fellow Buddhists. "In monasteries, bathing is a communal experience," she explains. The *zendo* may be years away from being realized, but she's already getting a little practice in sharing. "My boyfriend and I are both so attached to the soaking tub that we fight over tub time," she says, laughing. "My only regret is not installing a two-person version."

Opposite: Andrews chose wall-mounted faucets for the sink. "I prefer this to countertop versions, which clutter up the vanity and make it harder to clean."

set in stone

MIAMI architect René González has designed a number of art-related environments. In keeping with his belief that a room can be an intriguing art object in its own right, he designed a stunning, spa-like master bathroom for a pair of contemporary art enthusiasts in Florida. The architect turned the space into a three-dimensional, walk-in sculpture.

Instead of feeling constrained by this room's lack of natural light, González used it to his advantage. "We thought, Why not push the design in the other direction, to make the room feel internal, even contemplative, and turn it into a meditation room," he says.

González used recessed overheads along the ceiling, enhanced by fluorescent lights around the vanity. The tubes are placed vertically, like frames, in between large planes of mirror, to bounce light around the room. "Fluorescents are not unflattering if you position them to cast light from the side," he explains. "In a home, people and artwork should be lit the same way—in a diffused glow."

The toilet and bidet are hidden in a separate room toward the back, between the vanity and the walk-in shower. A curved soaking tub shaped like a hollowed-out river rock gently cups the body. González installed a glass shelf to one side to keep bathing accessories hidden from view.

Instead of a traditional handle, the shower's glass door pulls open via a cutaway edge for a more streamlined aesthetic. A pair of angled porcelain vessel sinks look more like sculptures than plumbing fixtures. The pared-down faucets above are placed at the exact edge where the marble backsplash and mirror meet. An oak stool and a woven basket for towels "bring in a rough-hewn quality against the sleek marble," says González.

The bath is the only room in the entire apartment not installed with art. "The room speaks for itself," he concludes.

The walls and the floor are clad in Italian Carrara marble, a favorite material of sculptors throughout the centuries. Architect René González carefully mapped out the placement of each slab so the prominent veins flow elegantly from one to another. The enormous walk-in bathing room has an oversize rain showerhead as well as standard wall-mount and handheld versions.

a star turn

"THIS WAS DINAH SHORE'S FUR CLOSET," says David Lee, opening the door to his cedar-lined sauna. Lee and his partner, Mark Nichols, live in a mod Palm Springs manse built for the songbird in 1963. A quick tour of the couple's airy master bath reveals few traces of the former inhabitant. No mink throws or chinchilla shrugs here—just sleek stainless-steel floor tiles, translucent glass walls, see-through sinks, and a Japanese soaking tub.

Lee, a TV producer, bought the house as a weekend getaway after being seduced by its history and its glass-wrapped modernist bones, credited to pioneering Palm Springs architect Donald Wexler. Lee set out to respect the mood of the existing design while bringing the house squarely into the present—especially the bathroom, which needed a complete renovation. "While I appreciated the period architecture— and, indeed, it was a selling point—I didn't want to live in a museum of midcentury modern," Lee says. So he called on architect D. Crosby Ross to make the space better suited to his twenty-first-century lifestyle, namely, his desire for spa-centric amenities like steam showers and saunas. "Crosby and I tried to give the bath the spirit of the rest of the home without being slavish to the period."

Ross knew his client's foibles well, having worked with this serial renovator on five projects over the course of many years—including a Scottsdale retreat and a house Lee built for his parents. "David is an active participant in the design process and always executes things on a large scale. He's quite adventurous and loves to be shocked and surprised," says Ross. "Yet he prefers simple luxuries—quality craftsmanship and a sense of tactility, like really plush towels and textured stainless-steel floor tiles." He ran with Lee's request that the house feel like a resort. "In one of our previous collaborations, David kept stressing that he wanted space and volume. So I said, 'Why don't we gut this whole thing and make it one large room that could

Previous pages, left: Ross designed a double-sided mirror to hang over the vanities. "I thought it would be fun to have someone brushing their teeth across from you, so you could see part of their body but not their face." Previous pages, right: The Japanese-style soaking tub, which has a sitting ledge inside, is made from stainless steel. Opposite: Slick materials such as glass tile and metal countertops are enhanced by textured surfaces like the wet area's poured-concrete floor.

be hosed down and dripped dry?'" Lee loved the idea: "I was tired of having to get into a little box to take a shower. I wanted the experience of bathing in a large, open space and this house seemed to yell for that sort of expansiveness."

Ross designed a wide-open room encircled by a series of water closets that house toilets, sauna, and steam shower. At the rear, a concrete-floored wet area with a rain showerhead and a soaking tub is backed by a full-height glass wall that slides open to the yard. The space features glass-tile walls and stainless-steel mosaic floors that stand up to water—and to the desert climate, whose heat and arid air combine with wild swings in temperature. "With such variations, you have to be cautious about material choices," Ross explains. Thus they used glass and steel for almost every surface, the sizes and finishes subtly varied—frosted to clear, brushed to chromed—to avoid repetition.

In the middle of the bathroom are dual vanities with boxy glass sinks on wengé wood bases. Above, a sleek double-sided mirror hangs from a structural beam piercing the skylight. "We cut a hole in the ceiling to pull natural light into the middle of the room and discovered the angled support beam hidden above," says Ross. "So I wired it for electricity and used it to mount a mirror for the vanities." He and Nichols, an interior designer, met as the renovation was wrapping up. "I designed the vanity for two as a what-if, and it ended up coming true," Ross jokes.

Both men, it turns out, love the bathroom's abundance of bathing options. "I envisioned a virtual water park in there—but sophisticated and stylish," says Ross. There's a sauna lined in minimalist cedar planks and a steam shower surfaced entirely in the same pale green glass tiles used throughout the main space. The architect also installed a stainless-steel soaking tub, which looks like a piece of sculpture. The rain shower wins the most raves. "When I stand under there, with the glass wall opened to the view of the mountains, it is otherworldly," says Lee. Nichols sheepishly admits to the occasional forty-five-minute shower. His preferred ritual is sitting peacefully in a plastic Verner Panton S chair, a cascade of water heating the concrete floor, the glass ajar. "I'd

Opposite: Lee and Nichols have one iconic piece of midcentury design in every room in the house. In the bathroom, it's the shower's injection-molded plastic Verner Panton S chair. Lined in the same glass subway tiles used throughout, a steam shower opens off the concrete-floored wet area. The space once housed former resident Dinah Shore's fur closet.

just leave that door open all the time, but then I'd get my wrist slapped for the electricity bill," he jokes. For occasions when the AC is on full blast and opening the wall is too much of an energy suck, Lee and Nichols can still take outdoor rinses: a palm tree on the terrace was converted into a shower. (The plumbing doesn't harm the tree since it grows from the top.)

There is nothing an architect loves more than a client who lives in a manner that's faithful to his design. Here, the home owners keep clutter, toiletries, and accessories to a bare minimum, letting the architecture shine. "David has always been meticulous and true to what's been designed for him," says Ross. "He definitely has a purist streak." Nichols elaborates: "If you're the kind of person who needs to see your toothbrush to remember to brush your teeth, this is not your kind of space. A certain informality comes with having all your loofahs and soaps out in the open—we don't have that here. The space is more of a Zen mind-clearing experience." In such minimalist surroundings, the challenge is to edit, edit, edit so that possessions are secondary to the sublime experience of space. According to Nichols, "It's important to be mindful and respectful of everything that comes to your world." Including a stunning piece of contemporary architecture tailored to your every desire.

Through renovating this house, Ross and Lee came to appreciate Donald Wexler's innovative use of materials, as well as his intelligent placement of glass to maximize views while still offering shading from the sun. They created interiors that they felt would be faithful to the original design in spirit—and they had an opportunity to see how good a job they did. "I was over at David's one day and there was a little knock on the door," Ross recalls. "I don't know why, but I had this weird premonition that it was Donald Wexler. We had communicated by phone—he still maintains an office downtown and had lent me some beautiful renderings of the home's original design. But I had never even seen a picture of him. I opened the door and looked at him and said, "I *know* you're Donald Wexler." David and I were excited to have him there—he was such a modest, humble, lovely gentleman.

And, best yet, he approved.

Opposite, clockwise from above left: The back-to-back vanities, which float clear glass sinks on cherrywood bases, are angled so they don't look like a big block in the middle of the room. A palm tree on the terrace was converted into a shower for outdoor rinses. Polygonal stainless-steel floor tiles have a subtle texture so they're slip resistant. Architect D. Crosby Ross designed a separate room for the toilet and the bidet, hidden behind frosted-glass wall partitions. The toilet and the urinal are stainless steel. "The toilet is a triumph of design over function," says David Lee. "It looks great but doesn't flush very well. And that is definitely an area where function needs to win out."

rhapsody in blues

BARCLAY BUTERA GUESSES THAT HE'S RENOVATED at least twelve homes of his own, from a midcentury modern Beverly Hills mansion to Frank Sinatra's former Twin Palms pad. At any one time, the jet-setting designer—and head of his namesake home-furnishings empire—presides over multiple residences scattered throughout the country. He's currently juggling two in California and one in Park City, Utah. "I am constantly buying and selling homes," says Butera. "As a designer, I like to explore many facets of living and many aesthetics—and dive into them completely. Each house has a different look."

These days, Butera spends most of his time at just one of his homes: a breezy 1950s cottage in Newport Beach, California. The property is a five-minute drive from his office and half a mile from the beach, and he treats it like a vacation home that he just happens to live in full-time—with a rotating cast of houseguests. Its style, appropriately, is seaside chic, with interiors that knit together a tranquil palette of aqueous blues with rustic, sandy textures like woven-raffia upholstery and sisal carpeting. Nautical accents abound: bowls of silver-plated shells, framed watercolors of sailboats, clusters of coral. "The look is 'over-the-top beach,'" he says, laughing.

Each part of the house riffs on the concept—especially the baths. "I spent a lot of time fussing over the design of the bathrooms here," he says. "While they are not overly grand—the main goal was to make good use of space—they are special and incredibly comfortable. I believe that baths are intimate retreats. It's important that they feel fresh and crisp and clean."

To make sure "crisp" didn't veer into "cold," he softened the expanses of bright white tile with strategic lighting. Above the vanity, he installed minimalist wall sconces chosen for their streamlined pharmaceutical look. The ceiling is also dotted with

Previous pages, left: The guest bedroom's kitschy lighthouse-print wallpaper heightens the seaside theme. "I thought it might be too juvenile, but people love it," says Butera. **Opposite:** In both bathrooms, Butera used boldly striped wallpaper. "I like the look of wallpaper and tile contrasting against each other," he says. "I prefer not to use vinyl because you don't get the same quality of color and line that you do in standard wall coverings. And as long as you ventilate properly, you don't need to use vinyl in wet areas."

recessed overheads attached to a separate dimmer for enhanced control. "I'm very conscious of lighting throughout the home," says Butera. "And I always keep a candle in each bathroom. It's much more atmospheric to dim the overheads and have soft, glowing candlelight—especially when you are entertaining."

One would be hard-pressed to find Butera in his bathtub: the designer confesses to being more of a shower enthusiast. He avoids rainfall fixtures ("they splash too much") in favor of oversize wall-mounted showerheads. "It's one of those simple details that make all the difference," he says. "People spend a lot of money trying to get a spalike bathroom, when just investing in a larger showerhead would do the trick." He does advise splurging on subtle details like beveling the edges of glass, as he did for the window-size mirror above his double vanity. "Beveling adds a level of sophistication and gives the piece a custom look."

Despite Butera's love of pattern play and strong color, it is unobtrusive, almost invisible elements like beveling that speak volumes about his refined yet casual take on luxury. He notes that the oil-rubbed bronze cabinet pulls don't match the nickel-finished faucets. "People get nervous about mixing finishes, but it personalizes the bathroom and makes it feel less decorated," he says. While he insists on mismatched hardware *within* a room, he's equally passionate about material continuity *among* all the bathrooms in a home. "Too many similar finishes next to each other looks matchy-matchy and a little contrived, but when walking through a house you want a feeling of unity. I almost always use the same stone countertop in the kitchen and baths, and the same faucets in every bathroom for consistency." Part of this reasoning is governed by common sense. "When I find a faucet that works well, I stick to it and use it over and over again. Life is so complicated outside the home, why not make it a bit simpler within?"

In the cottage's spunky guest bath, the same Carrara marble countertops, nickel faucets, and squared-off sinks used in the master suite become a neutral backdrop to a riot of color and whimsy. Because this room is used only for short visits, Butera dialed up the decor to completely immerse guests in seaside living.

Opposite, clockwise from above left: Nautical accents abound: bowls of silver-plated shells, framed watercolors of sailboats, clusters of coral. Prints of fish and seashells are framed in dark-stained wood with gold detailing. "I didn't worry about matching the finish of frames to the room's blue palette," says designer Barclay Butera. "It makes the rooms feel more 'real' this way—silver frames would have felt too contrived." The chair is seaside chic, with a tranquil palette of aqueous blues. Scented starfish are an inexpensive way to accessorize the bath. "They are porous so they'll hold fragrance longer," Butera explains. "Dry them out in the sun and spritz with perfume or linen spray."

"This room is a more playful take on the theme," he says. "I think visitors appreciate that element of surprise, that the house is not too seriously beachy." Stacks of plush ocean-colored towels are topped with starfish. A cut-crystal bowl holds natural sponges and shells he collected on the beach. (Butera's secret is to dry sea life in the sun and then spritz it with room freshener or perfume—"but keep it out of the shower at all costs, unless you want that sea-life smell.") Framed pastel prints of fish hang over eye-catching navy and turquoise stripes, which in turn play off the bedroom's lighthouse-print wallpaper. "You can see that I am a major wallpaper fanatic," he says. "People are afraid of taking design risks because they feel as if it's a permanent investment. But paint, wallpaper, and even hardware are all easy to change if you get sick of them."

The room is distinguished by mellow expanses of honed Carrara marble, white subway tile, hexagonal-tiled floors, and white-painted cabinetry with classic bead-board detailing. Butera mixed ceramic wall tiles with more luxurious statuary marble floors and counters to make the space feel upscale but still accessible. The hexagonal-shaped Carrara marble tiles cover the bath and shower floors, while the walls are clad in offset stacked subway tile alternating with straight-set 6-inch tiles for subtle variety.

The guest bath's beach-blanket decor is a crowd-pleaser. "Of all the rooms in the house, people love that one best," says Butera. "Whenever someone walks in there, they inevitably smile. It's a happy bath." But it's also deliberately timeless, like the rest of the house. "This is such a great space, so fresh and enduring. And while there's a level of luxury, everything in the house is livable and achievable. It's the first house I've owned that I can see myself growing older in."

Opposite: The large horizontal mirror above the double vanity is beveled for a more sophisticated look. Clean-lined light fixtures were chosen for their likeness to pharmaceutical tubing. Carrara marble counters are used in both bathrooms as well as in the kitchen. "I'm a firm believer in using the same countertops all throughout the house," says Butera. He prefers oversize wall-mounted showerheads. "I never use ceiling-mounted fixtures—the water explodes all over you. I prefer a more focused stream."

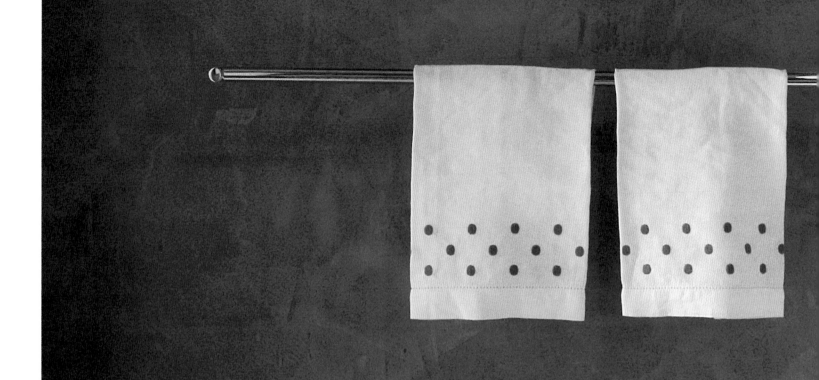

small spaces

Skinny, slim, snug, petite: whatever you call it, a small bathroom can be a *major* design challenge. How is it possible to fit a sink, a toilet, ample storage, and possibly a Jacuzzi in a tiny space and still have enough breathing room?

While small bathrooms are the norm in dense, space-challenged cities like Chicago and Los Angeles, they are not just an urban phenomenon. Indeed, while the size of the average American home grows to McMansion proportions, the percentage of space allotted to bathrooms doesn't always follow suit.

Of course, "small" is a relative term. To a suburban Atlanta home owner, 120 square feet may feel quite confined. To a New Yorker, 5 by 5 feet may be the point at which cozy veers to squashed. Small, then, is less about an actual, quantifiable measurement than about how that space needs to function, and in what context.

Through the ages, designers have adhered to one of two strategies to compensate for lack of square footage. Some choose to disguise diminutive confines by using mirrors or other optical illusions to make them appear larger (an age-old trick used even in a decidedly grand structure like Versailles). Others prefer to play up the smallness, like architect Frank Lloyd Wright, who deliberately designed almost claustrophobic vestibules and support spaces to make surrounding rooms feel larger. In either case, designers often delight in the opportunity size limitations can provide for risk taking and extreme creativity. After all, a designer has a captive audience in a small space—especially the bath.

Creative risk taking can translate to the use of bold hues and unusual materials that may be considered too daring for the more public areas of the home; a less-trafficked room is a particularly effective testing ground for such experimentation. While conventional wisdom discourages the use of bright colors in small spaces, it's often the first rule designers break. Jamie Drake, for example, drenched a small New York City bathroom in an intense turquoise. Far from making the space seem smaller, the wall-to-wall color visually expands the room. Architecture firm Workshop/APD lined every surface of a half bath in luxurious, buttery leather tiles that would have been impractical to use in a larger space or a more water-intensive master suite. The room is used mostly during dinner parties and social gatherings, so the owners felt liberated

Previous page: The walls and the ceiling are surfaced in a slightly reflective hand-troweled Venetian plaster in this bath, designed by Jamie Drake. The polished surfaces also add a touch of glamour—"which is especially desirable in a powder room," says Drake. **Opposite:** Stephanie Stokes designed this shower, which is surrounded by three walls of floor-to-ceiling mirror that reflects natural light from the small window opposite.

to do something aesthetically brazen. The clients are not alone: more plumbing and fixture manufacturers are cottoning to the trend of amped-up powder rooms, and have recently begun to design and market fixtures particularly for these spaces.

Pint-size quarters allow for the use of decorative elements that are best appreciated up close. Designer Maureen Wilson Footer adorned a powder room with painstakingly rendered paintings—minute accents that would have gotten lost in a larger room. Footer modeled the design on an eighteenth-century boudoir that was likewise quaint; she was inspired by how the small quarters intensified the effect of the illustrations.

One rule designers tend not to break when working with small spaces is sticking to one or two materials rather than mixing a number of finishes. Stephanie Stokes, for instance, used the same marble, limestone, and green slate tiles to line the floor and shower of a New York guest bath, but switched up the pattern from checkerboard to diamonds for visual variety. This pulls the eye from corner to corner, suggesting more expansive space—an effect enhanced by her clever use of mirrors. As the spare design proves, stick with two or three materials, smart built-ins, lots of glass—and big dreams.

hide and seek

"AN APARTMENT LIKE THIS DEMANDS A POWDER ROOM," says the owner of a newly modernized Manhattan prewar apartment. "Visitors expect to use a half bath—it's more elegant than a room with a tub, which always makes you feel as if you're sneaking into your host's master bathroom." Although he and his partner entertain often, they don't have many houseguests. So when renovating the apartment, they decided to convert the second full bath into a smaller one, and use the extra square footage for a media closet instead.

Matthew Berman and Andrew Kotchen of Workshop/APD redesigned the entire apartment to make the interiors more fluid and interconnected. "A prewar layout didn't work for our lifestyle," the owner explains. "We didn't want an apartment that rambled on with spaces we never went into. We asked them to line up the rooms so you could see into every one"—even the half bath.

Berman and Kotchen devised a more open floor plan that spirals around a wood-paneled box housing bathrooms, storage, and support spaces. Slipped between the master suite and living areas, the strikingly clean-lined box is a modern gesture within the otherwise classical context of wood floors and refurbished crown moldings. "We also thought it would be fun to create an otherworldly jewel box filled with unexpected materials. A powder room is a place to make a big statement to guests," says Kotchen. Adds the owner, "Since the room is used primarily during parties, we gave Matt and Andrew free rein to go nuts with the finishes. We wanted the design to be a surprise in every way."

The box itself is paneled in makore, a type of warm-hued African cherry with a graphic, striped grain. The architects lined the powder room in utterly luxurious leather tiles of a similar hue so that it appears to be an extension of the den. "The key to making small spaces feel cozy, rather than claustrophobic, is going crazy with just one material," says Berman. The textured tiles beg to be touched: "Leather has a

Previous pages, left: The flooring is Kirby slate, chosen as a dark anchor for the room's poppier elements. Previous pages, right: Wall tiles in rich leather balance the sleek sheen of a mod, stainless-steel toilet. Opposite: One wall of the powder room is given over to a custom light box depicting a lush rain forest. If the home owners grow tired of the image, it's easy to change—the light box is made from a replaceable photographic transparency sandwiched between glass and lit from behind by rows of dimmable fluorescent tubes.

reputation for being great in cold conditions, but the surface is just as divine on the hottest day," says the client. "The tiles have held up very well, with no peeling."

Indeed, the architects explain that the material is not as delicate as it looks. "I wouldn't recommend leather for a heavily trafficked master bath, but it's perfect for the walls of a powder room," says Berman. He and Kotchen were inspired by Philip Johnson's famed Glass House in Connecticut, where the renowned architect installed leather floors in his circular bathroom. "Using it on a bathroom floor is pretty adventurous and should probably be avoided," says Berman. Here, they grounded the room with dark squares of Kirby slate instead.

Other surprises include a stainless-steel toilet, which looks sleek and industrial at first glance. But the groovy fixture's reflective finish balances the rich walls. The custom sink is stainless steel, too, supported by a walnut storage cabinet. "We designed the sink to appear as if it were floating off the wall," says Berman. "The sense of levity makes the room feel bigger."

The vibrant greenery of neighboring Central Park inspired the bathroom's dominant feature: a wall-mounted light box that glows with the image of a mysterious, ethereal forest. "We bought the apartment for the views," says the owner. "The park inspired the interior design of the whole house—even in here." The powder room has its own large window offering a delightfully private twelfth-floor peek at the lush lawns below, and the architects thought it would be fun to somehow echo the view with an interior one. "We also wanted to light the space unconventionally, and came up with the light box—which illuminates from the side rather than from above," Berman explains. The light box is made from a photographic transparency sandwiched between glass and lit by rows of dimmable fluorescent tubes. The image—of an overgrown, "Hobbit"-like rain forest—plays off the more manicured park outside. The transparency is actually replaceable, and can be swapped if the owners desire a new look.

Guests here are transported from an urbane apartment to a hip but genteel downtown bar. "People just stand in there, mesmerized by the views," says the client.

Opposite, above: The powder room opens off the media room, which is paneled in makore, an African cherrywood with prominent patterning. The bathroom's leather walls are similarly colored, so that when the door is open, the bathroom looks like an extension of the media room.
Opposite, below: Architects Matthew Berman and Andrew Kotchen designed the custom sink's walnut cabinet to appear as if it were floating off the wall.

blue crush

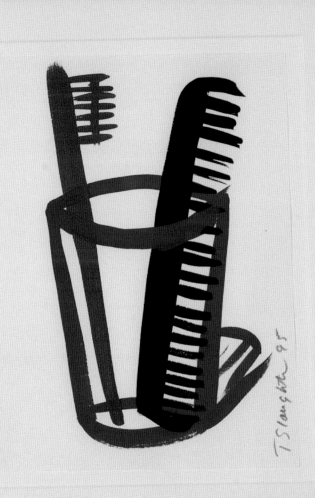

JAMIE DRAKE HAS DESIGNED HOT PINK BEDROOMS and citron sitting rooms, cherry red kitchens and rainbow-hued bathrooms. When Bari J. Mattes purchased her bachelorette pad in New York City's art gallery district, she knew just whom to call. "I had been in Drake's color-drenched Manhattan and East Hampton homes and loved them," she says. "Plus, we're friends, and I wanted to work with someone who got me."

The project's biggest challenge was sprucing up a serviceable but unremarkable space without subjecting it to renovation. Mattes's building was completed just a few months before she moved there in 2006. "Most clients are loath to gut brand-new construction. It's such a waste of money," says Drake. So how to make a superdeluxe space when you don't have the luxury of customizing every square inch—or, in the case of a small guest bath, ripping out the white-tiled tub and beige porcelain floors? "It becomes a matter of playing up strengths and toning down the weaknesses," he says.

Color went a long way to achieving both goals, largely by diverting attention away from the architecture—an undistinguished drywall box with little character and neutral finishes. Inspired by the client's collection of Murano glass, Drake designed her apartment around a full spectrum of blues, from frost to cobalt. "Jamie suggested the palette and I just fell for it," says Mattes. "I find it intense but still soothing—blue has that way about it." While most of the sunlit main living spaces feature icy aquas and subtle, watery hues, the designer picked a no-holds-barred turquoise for a spare bathroom. Walls and ceiling are awash in turquoise Venetian plaster. A reproduction antique chair is tarted up in turquoise crocodile-print leather. And the chenille shower curtain is splashed with cut-velvet flowers in—yes—turquoise. "The saturated color creates a visual exclamation point," Drake explains. "Bari definitely wanted to knock your socks off. Or, rather, your silk stockings—she is a very stylish lady!"

Previous pages: Covering all the surfaces in a single color blurs the edges of the room and makes it appear larger. Drake chose fabrics first, and then had the Venetian plaster hand-mixed for an exact match. **Opposite:** Since Bari Mattes uses her extra bath primarily as a powder room, she wanted to have it read as a small, enveloping space.

The deep blue bathroom debunks the myth that over-the-top hues make a room seem less spacious. "Slathering a small space in a strong color creates a special event," he says. "It can even erase boundaries and melt the edges of the walls to virtually expand a diminutive room." The reflective, polished Venetian plaster surfaces also lend a sense of depth and movement; it feels as if the room was carved from a block of turquoise stone. "This integral finish is more substantial than most wallpapers and adds a feeling of solidity to Sheetrock walls," says Drake. (It's water resistant, too.) "It's easier to match a paint to a fabric than vice versa, since fabrics come in fewer colors," he says. "I knew I wanted to use an intense turquoise in this space, but I didn't select the exact shade until after I picked the crocodile upholstery and the curtain fabric."

The room's focal point is the elegant swath of floral chenille-velvet. Detailed with a simple pinch pleat, the ceiling-mounted curtain "creates a fantastically theatrical wall of lushness within this small space," says Drake, "and disguises the full bath as a glamorous, sophisticated powder room." The curtain extends wall to wall to hide the built-in tub behind, including its surrounding white subway tiles. The fabric's taupe background also complements the beige porcelain floor tiles, integrating them into the decor so they recede into the background.

An existing cherrywood shelf above the sink has proved to be a convenient place to display artwork. The walls include highlights from Mattes's art collection, including a Paul Jenkins acrylic and a whimsical Weimaraner by William Wegman.

The crocodile-upholstered side chair is a decorative touch that's functional, too. "Conventional wisdom would say this room is too small for furniture," says Drake, "but this is my nod to an earlier time when all ladies' powder rooms had a place to rest a handbag." As an adviser to the mayor of Newark, New Jersey, Mattes has many occasions to dress up. Indeed, the room is a veritable extension of her dressing area across the hall. Pressed for closet space, Mattes installed a removable curtain rod in the rarely used tub from which to hang her ball gowns. Drake adds: "Of course, only her most glamorous gowns are secreted behind the velvet curtain."

Opposite: The pinch-pleated shower curtain is sewn from a voluptuous, luxurious cut velvet on a chenille background. "We lined it for extra fullness," says Drake. After Mattes moved in, she ran out of closets. So she installed a removable tension rod over the tub to gain additional hanging space. "I had no other choice!" she says. "I stash my ball gowns back there."

cargo space

"I ALWAYS DESIGN A BATHROOM TO BLEND IN with the surrounding decor, so when it's not in use you can keep the door open," designer Stephanie Stokes says. "Why hide it from view—especially if it's a little jewel box of a space?" A guest bath she designed for a Park Avenue pied-à-terre is certainly worthy of a close-up. Oil paintings hang from Venetian plaster walls, delicate sconces are topped with pleated muslin shades, and the painted wood vanity is crafted to look like an antique chest of drawers. Looking in from the adjacent library, one might guess that the room is a small salon.

It is, however, a bathroom, one that does triple duty as a powder room, a maid's closet, and a guest bath for the library, which is used as a spare bedroom. That meant sneaking in tons of storage plus a full-size shower, all within diminutive proportions. "It's ten by six feet, which is actually rather exciting for a New York prewar apartment—you should see some of the tiny spaces we deal with," says Stokes. "But sixty square feet is still very small." Her well-thought-out design allows the cozy space to multitask as efficiently as a galley kitchen, without compromising charm. Finishes have a pleasingly old-world texture, colors are deep and saturated, and the woodwork is as painstakingly detailed as it is in the rest of the apartment. "People think that you should treat bathrooms differently from living areas, and small spaces differently from large ones. But all you have to do is think a little harder—and more creatively," she insists.

One of Stokes's areas of expertise is storage, which she obsessively tailors around a client's particular belongings—from lingerie to appliances. Here, she designed a built-in L-shaped cabinet that hides existing plumbing lines and wraps around a small window, maximizing every square inch of space along two walls of the room. She chose a small undermount sink to preserve precious cabinet space below, freeing up enough room to include a built-in chest of drawers for visitors. There's even a cabinet to house cleaning supplies, including a compartment customized to the dimensions of the owner's Miele vacuum.

Previous pages: Venetian plaster, which is waterproof and easy to maintain, lines the walls. Wall sconces have pleated lamp shades made from muslin. "It's the only fabric I use in wet areas since it doesn't get water spots or discolor in the humidity," says designer Stephanie Stokes. Stokes altered the orientation of the floor tiles—squared-off in the shower, diagonal elsewhere—for visual variety. The painted wood vanity was designed to look like a freestanding bureau. The drawers below can be used as a dresser when guests stay over. Opposite, above: The teal and pumpkin color palette makes the room look like a continuation of the adjacent library. Opposite, below: The floor tiles in the shower are vertical, while the tile on the bathroom floor is horizontal, creating visual interest.

In addition to these spatial tricks, Stokes enlisted a few visual ones to create the illusion of elbow room. She altered the pattern of the floor tile—a mix of limestone, marble, and green slate—from square to diagonal for visual variety. The sprightly tiles pick up the teal and pumpkin scheme used in the rest of the apartment. Stokes advocates using strong hits of color in small spaces: "White does not make a space seem larger," she says. "Color gives your eye something to move over."

The walls of the petite room are Venetian plaster installed by New York artisan Stephen Balser of Art in Construction. Stokes loves to use the material in wet areas like kitchens and bathrooms. "Venetian plaster was developed in the Mediterranean to waterproof walls," she explains. "The finish lasts forever and is easy to maintain." It's also simple to clean—just wipe it down with a cloth. After using the material in myriad installations, Stokes has become finicky about the kind of plaster used. "For the walls, Stephen used a mix of sand, stone, paint pigments, and plaster that's not overly shiny. I prefer the natural plasters to the man-made acrylic varieties that are coming out of Italy, which I find too artificial looking. And, thankfully, the natural plasters are much easier to work with these days."

Stokes encourages clients to install a shower when space is limited—especially in less-used guest baths. "American manufacturers seem only to make supersize tubs. To get something that fits the proportions of a New York prewar apartment's bath, I sometimes have to fly bathtubs over from my secret source in England, which has a wider variety of smaller models to fit diminutive European bathrooms."

Here she installed a full-size shower, with mirrors on three sides. "Besides making the space look bigger, the reflective surfaces bring in extra daylight," she says. She installed towel rods that function as grab bars and a low threshold that keeps water from splashing into the main space but is still easy to step over. "It's safer for everyone. A wet shower can be a very dangerous place, no matter how beautifully appointed." Or intelligently designed.

Opposite: The bathroom transitions seamlessly from the living room. Stokes believes no room should hide from the rest of the decor.

museum quality

A LITTLE PARIS ON THE UPPER EAST SIDE is what Maureen Wilson Footer envisioned for her clients, worldly art patrons who purchased a flat in a Louis XVI–style apartment building. The structure was designed at the turn of the twentieth century by architect Horace Trumbauer, known for his grand French-inflected mansions. "The Beaux Arts limestone facade makes it look like a palace," says Footer. "The clients just fell in love with the whole gestalt of the place."

Although used as a schoolhouse for many years, the property had recently been sold and converted into apartments. Footer renovated the petite palace with an eye to restoring its French bones, which the developer had largely stripped away. "With the era of Louis XVI as our reference point, most of the interiors fell into place quickly," says Footer. "The limestone-clad foyer, boiserie in the living room, alcove beds— those features were automatic."

But she was unsure what to do with the ground-floor powder room. "It was the last room I designed," she says. "Because the room was a bit isolated from the main living spaces, I felt we could do something more visually intense."

Luckily, an eleventh-hour visit to the Metropolitan Museum of Art provided inspiration. Meandering aimlessly through the museum one day, she happened upon the Crillon Room. The octagonal boudoir from an eighteenth-century French mansion featured stunning Directoire boiserie paneling. The walls were hand-painted centuries ago with whimsical details: swirling vines, musical instruments, a gaily prancing field mouse. "The paneling made the room feel intimate. And while the painting was incredibly compelling, it was not overwhelming," says Footer. The scale, she decided, would translate well to the powder room's snug proportions. "That high level of decorative painting would be dizzying to re-create in a large space, but it was doable in smaller quarters."

Previous pages: Footer designed the vanity, which has a marble countertop and a neoclassical-style sink encircled with a gold band. Boiserie panels were washed with gray-green paint and then waxed. An Italian artist painted the motifs, which were inspired by the Crillon Room, a French Directoire period room at New York's Metropolitan Museum of Art. A hand-painted squirrel is a recurring motif along the walls' lower panels. The design is derived from Vaux-le-Vicomte, a mansion built by one of Louis XIV's financial ministers. **Opposite:** To make a New York powder room seem more glamorous, designer Maureen Wilson Footer alternated boiserie with mirrored panels faux-aged with both gold and silver undertones.

She outfitted the elegant room with marble floors, crystal sconces, and a neoclassical-style vanity. Delicate boiserie, washed with gray-green paint, clads all four walls and even the door. Each panel is embellished with miniature urns, intertwined vines, and other dainty flora and fauna, all modeled on imagery from the Crillon Room. The fanciful decorations were executed by an Italian artist, who Footer says "really devoted himself to the project, constantly running back and forth between the apartment and the Met to check details."

Along the way, they took a few liberties with the imagery. The wife felt that the Crillon Room's mouse motif should be replaced by a more, well, *approachable* critter. So they chose a squirrel instead, based on a detail at the historic French mansion Vaux-le-Vicomte. The pan-flute and violin motifs on the door were also personalized. "Like the clients, the artist was a serious amateur musician, so he included a few bars of his favorite Bach fugue on the sheet music," Footer says. "You'd have to be a real music buff to get the reference, but the artist's input was one of those little grace notes to the room."

To make the space seem bigger, Footer alternated the boiserie with stretches of faux-aged mirror. "Mirrors are wonderful illusionistic devices," she explains. "Here, we used both gold and silver undertones to create the faux-aged effect. Silver can be so harsh when used alone; gold softens it a little, giving a nice warm patina." The faucets, the vanity legs, and even the light-switch covers have a gold finish, as do the crystal wall sconces brought over from the clients' former residence.

On the floor, gray-veined white marble is inset with contrasting bands of green. "We chose the green marble because it had a nice pink vein," says Footer. The green marble boxes appear to divide the room into two zones: one housing the toilet, the other housing the vanity. "We segmented the room using the wall pilasters and the floor geometries," Footer explains. "In addition to making the space seem larger, it added a sense of architectural distinction that the developers had stripped away."

Indeed, there's very little sense that this charming chamber was once a bland box. "The room is done up to the nines," says Footer. Just walking into this room makes guests feel like they are, too.

Opposite, above: Crystal wall sconces come from the clients' previous home. Their back plates have a similar rosette detail to the one Footer had chosen to accent the wall panels. **Opposite, below:** The faucets have a gold finish to create a faux-aged effect.

entertaining

The most popular destination on today's party circuit is not a New York City nightclub or a celebrity-studded LA dive bar. The talk of the town is the master bathroom, surprising as that may sound.

The private sanctuary for showering and primping would seem a place ill suited to drinking cocktails and nibbling canapés. But communal bathing is an age-old tradition that transcends cultural boundaries, from Turkish hammams to Russian bathhouses. Indeed, the communal bathhouse has been reborn as the upscale home spa—as in a young couple's home in rural Connecticut, for which architecture firm Poesis designed a 25-yard indoor pool, a hot tub, and a six-person sauna that's been the site of many girls' nights.

For some social butterflies, it's a short leap from showering in the company of others to inviting company to sip martinis near the shower. The intriguing phenomenon indicates that as people live more casually, the boundary between private and public areas gets blurred—and this once secreted-away room continues its swift march into the foreground of the home.

These days, people often use their bathrooms for entertaining because they are making the most of every inch of the home. Style setters Jason Oliver Nixon and John Loecke, for instance, renovated the top floor of their Brooklyn town house into an open-plan bath that connects to a lovely terrace with stunning views. The couple thought it would be a shame to reserve the space only for themselves—who would give up the opportunity to entertain on the deck?—so they kitted out the adjacent bath like a living room. When guests pass through en route to dinner on the terrace, they don't feel as if they're in the couple's loo. It seems a few taboos still hold: guests will party in a bathroom, but they don't want to *feel* as if they're in a bathroom.

The room, of course, is used either for bathing *or* for partying, but not both at the same time—a key aspect of the entertaining bath. Similarly, Benjamin Noriega-Ortiz's scheme for an outgoing Chicago couple centers on a sculptural sink that

Previous pages: The firm Poesis designed a skylit octagonal cupola that filters in Connecticut sunshine. The pool is enclosed by mahogany-framed windows and two walls of French doors, which can be opened so the space feels like an extension of the yard. The decking is Ipé slats, with drainage below. The walls are lined with low-maintenance subway tile. **Opposite:** Miles Redd's own bathroom doubles as a dressing room; the mirrored doors along the entrance wall disguise Redd's closets. The walls around the tub are book-matched marble, part of the original design. The shower, like the vanity and the sink, is illuminated by backlit glass ceiling panels.

converts from shaving hub to champagne bar—just remove a mirror, fill the trough with ice, and voilà. (Sounds like good clean fun.) The multitasking design encourages visitors to wander the entire apartment during bashes and not just crowd into the living areas. But even the owners have been stunned by how long people linger there, reveling, apparently, in the novelty of the environment.

After all, guests love nothing more than to be wowed by an unusual setting, the impetus for Miles Redd's party bath. The decorator has plenty of glamorously appointed rooms to host soirees in his East Village town house. But on special occasions he throws dinner parties in the mirror-paneled master bath. The space, a 1930s boudoir salvaged from a David Adler estate, is a truly magical milieu when the lights are dimmed and candles lit. Redd wanted to share it with others—and who cares that it's a bathroom so long as it's a fabulous space.

People today want the best for the bathroom: the best location in the house, the most luxurious decor, the grooviest sink. Why keep all that hidden—indeed, why not bring in the party?

having it both ways

FOR A YOUNG COUPLE LIVING IN NORTHWEST CONNECTICUT, building their dream home meant reconciling two opposing desires. On one hand, they envisioned a tranquil, relaxing dwelling in which to decompress from their stressful media careers. On the other, they wished to entertain often—hosting everything from adult ski weekends to parties for their two kids—and needed a space that could accommodate a full house.

Architecture firm Poesis, based just a few towns away in Lakeville, Connecticut, answered both wishes with a thoughtful design that supports group fun and solo retreat in equal measure. For introspective lounging, there's a secluded master bath. Slipped into the most private, faraway corner of the house, the sanctuary has its own deck and a soaking tub with gorgeous views of the backyard pond and wildflower garden, creating the feel of a private tree house.

For more extroverted fun, there's a boisterous ground-floor spa wing, with a six-person sauna, a steam shower, a hot tub, and even a 25-yard indoor lap pool. "If you're building your dream house in snowy northern Connecticut, a home spa is at the top of your wish list," says Pilar Proffitt, who runs Poesis with her husband, Rob Bristow. "Winters here are rough. The area has been dubbed the 'icebox' of Connecticut— you can have three feet of snow in your yard until April. You get stuck inside for weeks on end. So it's paradise to have a large house with all these amenities at your disposal. The family can throw a pool party for fifty kids, or host a ski trip and then unwind with a few friends in the sauna."

Both spaces are adorned with warm, unmannered finishes and quietly luxe materials like honed marble and finely grained woods. "The clients hired us when the place was in sticks," says Proffitt. "The structure was already built, but the interiors were not figured out at all. Giving a big house like this a sense of quality meant minimizing the impression of vastness. I am all for large spaces, but you can feel lost in them. We

Previous pages: In the ground-floor spa wing, the six-person sauna and adjacent shower, behind the frosted-glass wall, are wrapped in cedar. The steam shower's frosted-glass walls filter in light while affording privacy when the sauna is also in use. Cedar siding wraps the exterior of the sauna for a warm, lodgelike ambiance. **Opposite:** Also in the spa wing, antique chairs and an armoire create a furnished feel in the sauna/shower room. Tiled wainscoting behind the custom washstand folds back to form a shallow ledge for toiletries. Simple fluorescent strips on either side of the mirror are an elegant yet practical lighting solution.

were attentive to surface textures and divvied up rooms into smaller zones to create a sense of scale."

In the master bath, that meant treating each plumbing fixture like its own little room and keeping the rest of the space airy. Opening off the master bedroom lounge through sliding mahogany doors, the hushed oasis has a dramatically sloped ceiling and enormous mahogany-framed windows. To enhance the feeling of uncluttered spaciousness, the soaring room is sparsely furnished—just a bright orange molded-fiberglass Eames chair and a weathered child's chair below a trio of walnut shelves. Expansive stretches of organic materials—walnut floors, plaster walls—are perked up by planes of colorful mosaics. "We wanted to ground the space, so we used a lot of wood and kept the palette quite limited," says Proffitt.

She designed the room like an art gallery, treating the sinks, tub, and toilet like sculptures by enveloping them in glass mosaics. "We used very expensive tile but in limited locations to create more of a composition," she explains. A drop-in soaking tub is surrounded by a boxlike blue-tiled platform, which doubles as a seating ledge and a shelf for soaps. The double vanity, supporting a pair of cubist sinks, is tucked into a cove lined in green tile; walnut drawers below blend with the floors. In the far corner of the room, the toilet and the bidet are grafted to the wall with a stretch of celadon-hued mosaics. The bands of color pop against the Venetian plaster walls, smoothed over with a high-polish, troweled finish. "When I use tile, I gravitate to planes of color—it's more like painting a canvas," says Proffitt.

The lively tile boxes also play off the honey-toned woods. The walnut floor was the key to making the lofty surroundings seem less vast and more furnished—but the architect was almost talked out of it. "I was cautioned about installing a wood floor in a wet space. The wood guy tells you one thing, the contractor tells you another, and all the data is conflicting. Sometimes you have to weigh the pros and cons and make up your own mind," says Proffitt. Thanks to three coats of waterproofing, the floor has held up well over time.

The shower, located at the far end of the room, is lined in crisp white marble tiles inset with a swath of

Opposite, above: The dramatic sloping ceiling gives the master bathroom the appearance of a tree house. Walnut floors and mahogany windows make the room feel warm and comfortable, as does a vintage Eames fiberglass chair and framed artwork. The toilet and the bidet are backed by green glass mosaic wainscoting installed in a brick pattern for variety. **Opposite, below:** The spa wing bathroom, which has both a toilet and a bidet, can be closed off from the adjacent shower/sauna space. Two staggered rows of stainless-steel pegs for towels, robes, and swimsuits let this part of the bathroom double as a changing room.

green mosaics to accentuate the steeply angled ceiling. The lofty oasis has two benches and two showerheads controlled by handles near the entrance so the owners don't get wet when they adjust the water. The only thing missing is a door. "The clients wanted to partition the shower with a glass wall, but I told them that they didn't need to. It's large enough that water doesn't splash out on the wood floor, and it's so heavenly that you can just walk into this gigantic, private bathing room, with its own windows. Although I might not have designed it this way myself—the builder placed the shower at this end of the room—I love that it feels so tucked away."

While the master bath's shower overtakes the most remote corner of the entire house, the spa wing is located at its heart and soul. The wing wraps around the summer entrance hall, leading into the kitchen and living room. "It's nice that these two wings flow so easily into each other, because that's how the owners use the house. After skiing, everyone migrates to the hearth between the kitchen and living areas, then winds up in the spa."

It was important for the spa to be not only integrated with the regular ebb and flow of the house but also stylistically compatible. The pool room, for instance, is ringed by the same mahogany-framed windows and doors used throughout; in warmer months, the doors can be flung open. A skylighted octagonal cupola at the room's midpoint reiterates the home's modern-farmhouse quality while breaking up the vast ceiling. The pool is traced in slate coping bordered by Ipé wood decking, whose warm yellow tones melt pleasingly into the mahogany portals. The rich wood is offset by cream-colored subway-tile walls, which withstand splashing kids and the spray from the open shower at the pool's west end. Also at this end of the pool is a rectangular hot tub deep enough to stand in, with wraparound seating so a large group can relax together.

After a vigorous swim, guests can repair to the steam shower in the adjacent spa, which is more intimately proportioned. "For the size of the house, the spa is surprisingly small; it's actually two rooms in one—the sauna and the shower are grouped together, and the toilet is off in its own room," explains Proffitt. "The

Opposite: The master bath's generous shower has two showerheads, plus built-in seating on both sides. The shower's back wall is inset with a swath of forest green mosaics that accentuate the angle of the ceiling line above.

builder made a huge entryway, which ate up some of the space that could have been devoted to a bigger spa." She played up the cozier dimensions with slightly warmer textures than those used upstairs, while repeating the same white plaster walls, mahogany windows, and walnut floorboards. Instead of slick colored-glass tile, she used matte off-white marble to line the bathroom walls and the steam shower. "The material has a really great texture—honed but still bright white. It's almost like a pumice stone," says Proffitt. She clad the six-person sauna inside and out with horizontal cedar slats, which extend all the way to the shower's frosted-glass wall. Reminiscent of a modernist ski lodge, the cedar siding softens in the late-afternoon light. The shower, meanwhile, is large enough to double as a changing room. Frosted glass along one side filters light into the shower yet is opaque enough to afford privacy when the sauna is also in use.

Proffitt encouraged the owner to furnish the sauna/steam shower room with antiques so it feels more like an extension of the living room than a typical bathroom. "They moved from a larger house in California and had a warehouse full of furniture. We had to find a home for everything, and many pieces wound up here." A large armoire reposes near the steam shower, while antique side chairs perch by both sinks. Even the washstand was designed to look more like furniture than a built-in, with a footed walnut base and tiled wainscoting that folds back to form a shallow ledge for toiletries.

The hub of the spa is a warm, walnut-floored powder room with doors leading in from the sauna and the summer foyer. A side wall anchoring the toilet and the bidet is lined with the same white marble as the steam shower, sliced by a walnut ledge displaying artwork. Proffitt installed a series of stainless-steel pegs so the space can be used as a dressing room. "It's the powder room for the ground floor, so we wanted to keep it separate from the sauna but still connected to it. Both spaces can be used as locker rooms at the same time." Like the dressing room of a chic boutique, this simple, light-filled space invites guests to shed their clothes—and their inhibitions—and slip on a swimsuit to join in the fun.

Opposite, above: In the master bathroom, a drop-in tub is surrounded by a boxlike platform surfaced in blue glass mosaics. His-and-hers sinks with wall-mounted taps rest on a countertop surfaced in green glass mosaics. For a streamlined look, architect Pilar Proffitt installed a band of mirror above the sink rather than a medicine cabinet. Storage is relegated to walnut drawers and cabinets below. Opposite, below: The soaking tub in the master bathroom overlooks the backyard pond and wildflower gardens. "The room faces southeast, so there's plenty of light throughout the day," says the client. A spa rack is a practical accessory for such a large tub; the wide ledge also has plenty of room to hold toiletries. A floor-mounted towel warmer is easily reachable from both the sinks and the soaking tub.

shine on

NEW YORK decorator and creative director of Oscar de la Renta's home collection Miles Redd is known for glamorous, debonair interiors steeped in decorative arts history.

So it is no surprise that Redd's master bathroom, on the top floor of a genteel 1826 Greenwich Village town house, gives a nod to bygone days. The room, paneled in floor-to-ceiling mirror, was designed by David Adler in the 1930s as the lady's boudoir of a grand estate in Lake Bluff, Illinois. "I found it at a salvage yard in Chicago," Redd says, still incredulous at his discovery.

Redd got the chance to buy the room in its entirety—book-matched marble bathtub, squared-off crystal door levers, Directoire paneling, and all. The room's layout is identical to its former incarnation: square in plan, with one fixed element on each wall. A portal beside the sink leads into a whimsical toilet room lit by a shell-shaped chandelier and tented in striped blue linen to match Redd's bedroom.

He chose the wallpaper to mimic silver leaf. The sink's marble backsplash was replaced with mirror to mesh more seamlessly with the surrounding paneling. The floor is new, too, a modernized take on the room's original black terrazzo, which was embellished with a dainty leaf pattern. To create a more gentlemanly look, he instead chose inky marble slabs inset with steel slivers. "The slabs were so big that we had to hoist them through the window," recalls Redd.

Redd has used the glamorous room to host candlelit dinners. He's found that guests love the intrigue of eating in such a compelling and unusual environment: "There's nothing like being in a mirrored room filled with candle-light. And, after a few glasses of wine, you don't even notice it's a bathroom."

The floor-to-ceiling mirrored panels of decorator Miles Redd's bathroom were designed by renowned classicist architect David Adler in the 1930s for the Armour family in Lake Bluff, Illinois.

raising the bar

OVERWHELMED BY TWELVE-HOUR WORKDAYS and frequent business trips, hardworking professionals Marty Yee and John Brill decided to trade their 4,000-square-foot suburban Chicago home for a smaller, more manageable pied-à-terre. Downsizing, in this case, actually meant upgrading. Located in the heart of the Golden Mile, the couple's 1,200-square-foot apartment is on the twenty-first floor of a posh five-star hotel that offers residents access to guests' amenities like maid and room service. "I don't think we could have the lifestyle we do without those amenities at our disposal," says Brill. "The condo has its own concierge and a fantastic staff, from doormen to engineers. The range of services is amazing—they'll arrange our dry cleaning and even furniture deliveries. And with a health club downstairs, I no longer have an excuse to skip the gym. It was worth giving up a little square footage for such conveniences."

One thing Yee and Brill weren't willing to give up, though, was their social life—namely, a fondness for entertaining at home. "Marty and John are famous for throwing amazing parties," says Benjamin Noriega-Ortiz, who designed the apartment's interiors. He would know: Noriega-Ortiz and Yee are old friends from their post-college days, and have logged plenty of time lounging in each other's homes. "They entertained all the time in their old house. So when they decided to move, I worked to re-create that party spirit in the new place."

The main challenge he faced was contending with a much smaller canvas. The couple's former bathroom, for instance, was a lofty 20 by 30 feet—almost half the size of this entire apartment. Here, the master bath was petite, hardly big enough for two people to brush their teeth together. "To gain enough room to expand the bath meant borrowing space from an adjacent hallway leading to the bedroom," says Noriega-Ortiz. He suggested doing away with the corridor altogether and combining both

Previous pages, left: Benjamin Noriega-Ortiz designed a custom white acrylic mirror to separate the long trough sink into a two-person unit; the skinny side is oriented to the bathroom door so it seems to disappear. The mirror can be removed so the trough sink can be used as an ice bucket for parties. **Previous pages, right:** Noriega-Ortiz used the same variety of green-tinged vanilla marble to line the floor, the shower, and the sink countertop to make the space look like an outdoor courtyard. The custom vanity was designed to look like a sculptural fountain. The unit floats a 44-inch-long stainless-steel trough on a 36-inch lacquered wood base. **Opposite:** The sink's cream-colored lacquered base has three open shelves facing the shower, which are used to store toiletries.

spaces—and both functions—into one, converting the bathroom into a sort of courtyard entry to the sleeping area. The clients loved the idea and the new dimensions, which doubled the size of the bath. "The original floor plan had too much hallway and the master suite seemed closed off," says Yee. "By combining the two and downsizing the master bedroom slightly, Benjamin maximized both a real and a perceived sense of space."

The room now feels less like a bath than a grand, gardenlike foyer. To begin with, there is no actual door, just a wide doorway draped in billowy translucent parachute nylon. "I eliminated as many walls and doors as possible to take advantage of every square inch," says Noriega-Ortiz. "Since Marty and John have no kids—and very rarely host houseguests, now that they have a hotel downstairs—privacy isn't a major concern." (The drapes also hide floor-to-ceiling medicine cabinets.) To the left of the entrance is a pair of frosted-glass doors, one leading to the walk-in closet, the other to the WC. Straight ahead is the shower, almost invisible behind a glass wall. "An open bathroom is liberating for designers. You just install a bathing area and a separate toilet room and the rest is up for grabs to do whatever your heart desires," says Noriega-Ortiz.

The bathroom floor is lively vanilla marble, whose lime green tinge gives the space the verdant presence of an outdoor patio. Noriega-Ortiz lined the shower with the same stone so it reads like an accent wall rather than a boxed-in wet space; squint and you don't even notice the showerheads or the recessed shelving in the side walls. A large bathing area was the clients' top priority. "Our old bath had a whirlpool tub that took up the center of the room, and a huge steam shower, which we loved," says Brill. The couple's new shower is a little more modestly sized, but still has enough room for two. "I've found that couples these days are so busy that when they are actually at home together, they like to be with each other every waking minute. So many of my clients tell me that the shower is their place for catching up," says Noriega-Ortiz.

In the middle of the space is a sculptural vanity that balances a stainless-steel trough sink on a circular lacquered base. "It looks like an outdoor fountain that

Opposite: The door from the living areas to the bathroom is screened by translucent nylon curtains, which hide medicine cabinets.

you'd find in the courtyard of a Mediterranean villa," says the designer. He had the inspired if unusual idea to design a sink that could double as a wet bar, so the room could be put to use during the couple's frequent bashes. "It was my strategy to encourage guests to use the whole apartment and not just crowd into the living areas," he says. During the day, the trough sink, which has a faucet on either end, is a double vanity. (A trio of shelves below, facing the shower, stashes toiletries out of view.) At night, filled with bottles of Veuve Clicquot and Prosecco, it's a wine bucket; the white acrylic mirror can be removed and stowed away. "The multitasking sink looks like a piece of sculpture, yet it's practical," says Noriega-Ortiz.

Brill admits that they didn't use the sink as intended during their housewarming party, and guests jammed into the living area. "But during all of our subsequent parties, we filled the sink with ice and champagne and placed glasses on the countertop. There's a full bar on the counter between the kitchen and the dining room, but you can only get champagne here. The bathroom became a gathering place, just like people would congregate around any bar. I didn't expect that people would hang out in there, but they do. It's hysterical what a popular space it's become."

Although the couple's apartment may be an extreme example, Noriega-Ortiz has noted a trend to larger, more decorated bathrooms that double as living and socializing areas. And not just for space-challenged, party-centric urbanites who like to use the whole house for entertaining—it's a phenomenon embraced by young families, too. The bathroom, he argues, is turning into what the kitchen once was: the family hub, and a place in which to invest. "Because this is a room you really engage with multiple times a day, people don't think twice about spending a ton of money on gadgets and expensive faucets. The high-tech Toto toilet has become the new Sub-Zero refrigerator."

And the bath has become the new nightclub.

Opposite: A pair of frosted-glass doors to the left of the entrance leads to a walk-in closet and to an adjacent private toilet room.

entertainment value

"MOVING TO BROOKLYN WAS THE BEST THING WE'VE EVER DONE," says Jason Oliver Nixon. "We love having a backyard, two decks, and a three-story brownstone—all for less than the selling price of our Manhattan one-bedroom." And, best of all, the new home base affords ample room and opportunity to entertain.

The brownstone, for all its charms, did have one major drawback. The top floor housing the master bedroom was cramped and lacked a bathroom. Luckily, the home owners have a strong sense of vision. Nixon is a style director for luxury-lifestyle magazines; his partner, John Loecke, is an interior designer; both moonlight as writers. Together, they mapped out a plan to rework the floor's oversize staircase landing into a bathroom, tearing down the back wall of the house to connect the space to a newly built rear terrace. The multitasking room now doubles as a private master bath and a public sunporch. "The best view in the house is from this terrace—we look out onto sunny open gardens and faraway Brooklyn apartments. It would have been a shame to make this space off-limits during parties," Loecke explains.

To create a loungey feel, they hid the bath fixtures in plain sight. A curved-leg mirrored vanity appears to be an elegant console. The minimalist loo, with its hidden plumbing, could be mistaken for a cylindrical stool or side table. The penny-tiled shower turns its back to the staircase, so it's almost invisible upon entry. "When we began renovating, we discovered that the plumbing already ran to the third floor, so there must have been a bathroom here at one time. Thankfully, that made it much easier to convert the space into a wet zone," says Loecke.

The rest of the decor is sophisticated prepster-chic, an ode to the graphic, retro glamour of society decorator Dorothy Draper: punchy lime green walls, white-painted floors, framed artwork, a wicker reading chair decked out in a bright 1940s botanical print. "I love how Draper mixed theatrical flourishes with wonderful color, bringing a stylized yet accessible quality to her interiors. We wanted lots of drama

Previous pages: The shower is lined with blue and white penny tiles and white hexagonal floor tiles. The all-weather Asian garden stools move from here to the patio as needed for extra seating or surface area. Marble slabs protect the white-painted floors from water damage below the minimalist toilet and shower. **Opposite:** The shower is oriented away from the stairs so it's hidden from view, inviting some measure of privacy in a room with no doors.

and impact here, so she was the perfect inspiration," says Nixon. They even purchased some of her vintage furnishings, including a cabinet that stores toiletries and high-design bric-a-brac. "Thanks to eBay, we've been able to stock up on numerous pieces from her España collection—at amazingly inexpensive prices. This cabinet was only two hundred fifty dollars, probably because the hardware was missing."

Personalized with graphic wallpaper lining and inexpensive faux-coral pulls from Anthropologie, it's certainly not your traditional medicine cabinet. "We treated the bathroom as a living area," says Loecke. "Thus we didn't want built-in cabinets and had to be creative about storage units." To create continuity with the lower two floors, the couple also repeated many of the same fabrics and finishes used in other rooms. The cabinet's sprightly geometric wallpaper, for instance, brightens up the master bedroom. The penny tiles in the shower are also used in the kitchen. Says Nixon, "Why should a bathroom be furnished differently from any other room?"

And why should indoors be furnished differently from outdoors? The couple used all-weather accents for both the terrace and the bath. The composite-wood deck is scattered with outdoor chaise lounges pepped up with pillows covered in cheery water-resistant fabrics—which withstand parties and postshower lounging alike. "Nothing beats taking a steam with the French doors wide open, then relaxing on the terrace in a robe with the morning coffee," says Nixon. "It's as close as you can get to having an outdoor shower in this city." The couple also notes how daylight dances through the room all day long, reflected by the mirrored vanity. Nixon loves the vanity for its connotations of glamour, too: "It feels very Nick and Nora Charles. Brushing my teeth at that sink makes me want to sip a martini."

Which he has, in fact, done, since the vanity becomes a makeshift wet bar during parties. "It's really magical to host parties on the terrace as the sun is setting," says Loecke. "When entertaining," says Nixon, "we create a sort of modern riff on a Victorian terrarium by filling up the shower with ferns."

Watering hole indeed.

Dorothy Draper

Nixon and Loecke are unapologetic fans of Dorothy Draper, the self-taught decorating and lifestyle doyenne who rose to fame in the 1930s and '40s. Nixon first discovered what he calls "Draperama" when he moved to New York City and met the decorator's successor, Carleton Varney, who took over Draper's firm after she died. "Carleton introduced me to the full scope of her genius," he explains.

Draper was known for her modern, no-holds-barred approach to colors, adorning her interiors with oversize prints and high-energy, graphic punch. Indeed, one of the couple's favorite Draperisms is "Banish the beige." "So as you look around the bathroom, you see bold blues, bright greens, whites, reds, and browns everywhere, from tiles to lamp shades," says Nixon.

For all the visual intensity Draper brought to her projects—which included interiors of the Carlyle and Greenbrier hotels—she was noted for using furniture with clean silhouettes, especially updates of classical antiques. The domestic diva also wrote decorating how-tos, as well as a witty primer on party throwing, the recently reprinted *Entertaining Is Fun!: How to Be a Popular Hostess.* The 1941 tome instructs readers how to entertain in a high-style way that suits their artfully decorated homes—which could also explain Nixon and Loecke's unabashed affection for her.

Previous page: Multicolored penny tiles line the wall behind a mirror-paneled vanity, designed by Barbara Barry. The tall glass-fronted cabinet is a vintage Dorothy Draper design, updated with faux-coral pulls. A jaunty green-and-white geometric wallpaper—also used in the adjacent master bedroom—lines the back of the glass-doored cabinet, creating continuity between the two spaces. Right: The terrace at the back of the house is surprisingly private. "It's surrounded by low-rise buildings—so no need for curtains on the French doors," says Nixon. A vintage gourd-shaped lamp and a starburst mirror perk up the white-on-white storage cabinet. Embellished with a subtle leaf pattern, the unit doubles as a bar for parties.

his, hers, and theirs

AS OFTEN AS THEIR HECTIC SCHEDULES ALLOW, Diane and Craig Soloman escape from Manhattan to their breezy Sagaponack, New York, weekend home with their two kids and as many friends and relatives as they can gather. The stately but relaxed house, which the couple built from the ground up, is tailor-made for entertaining, with large living areas, plenty of sleeping space, a pool house with a kitchen and massage tables—and a vibe that's utterly laid-back and welcoming. "Before we built this, we lived in a smaller house on the property," explains Diane Soloman. "I was so relaxed those summers because I knew I'd be tearing down the house—I didn't even care if someone spilled a drink or damaged the furniture. It dawned on me to strive for that same easygoing casualness here."

"Casual" is a mantra for Paul Siskin, the Solomans' longtime interior designer. His forte is soft-spoken, unpretentious spaces that take a backseat to the family activity unfolding within. "Diane and Craig wanted the house to be beautiful but not at all precious," he says. "It's a 'wow' house for sure, but every finish was chosen to be livable and durable. They plan to use the house for a long time." Adds Soloman, "The interiors needed to be useful right now and work for the long haul, too."

Planning for the future, she asked Siskin for an enduring design that would wear well over many decades and comfortably accommodate multigenerational living, particularly in the pool house, which is command central in the summer. To accommodate the swell of visitors, Siskin designed a chic, multiuse guest bathroom.

Husband and wife each have their own bath, too, along the hallway to the master bedroom. "Both rooms are big but, like the rest of the house, they're timelessly appointed and really not so grand," says Siskin. Diane's in particular was conceived for function rather than self-indulgence. "I don't spend a ton of time lounging around

Previous pages: Craig Soloman's bathroom is striped in alternating bands of limestone and beige marble. One corner of the room is given over to a midcentury Danish china cabinet made from exotic rosewood. Limestone and marble wall stripes continue into the toilet area opening off the shower. Because it's not a shared bathroom, privacy was not such a big issue here. There are three showerheads: handheld, rainfall, and wall-mounted versions. Designer Paul Siskin converted a 1960s rosewood cabinet into a vanity by adding a limestone top. The piece had a hole in the back when he purchased it, which accommodated the plumbing lines. **Opposite:** In the pod house bath, Siskin included numerous racks and pegs to hang clothes and bathing suits so the bath could double as a changing room. The walls are lined in rectangular white-porcelain tiles.

my bathroom," she says. "I kind of get in and get out. I asked Paul for something calm and peaceful and practical." He dreamt up an airy, hushed room with dark-stained wide-plank floors and wood-paneled walls painted soothing cream. "A wood bath is unusual, but I find the material to be much warmer than tile," she says. "And, since it's only me using the space, I didn't have to worry about water splattering." (The plush, tonal fleur-de-lis-print area rug takes care of postshower spillage.)

The focal point of her room is a voluptuous freestanding tub with an undulating profile. "I installed it because I thought perhaps one day I'd take a bath," she jokes. "But I haven't used it yet. I've never really understood baths: you wait for the water to fill up, then you hop in and what do you do? It gets cold after ten minutes." Siskin admits that the decision to install a bathtub was motivated by a vague sense of obligation; even for a couple who intends to keep their house forever, the concept of resale value still looms large.

Other than the tub, the room is sparsely furnished: an antique silver-leaf vanity mirror, a metal console made from a vintage armor box, and pieces from the Solomans' growing art collection. Siskin's guiding philosophy is to include enough white space for clients to personalize their homes after his work has been completed.

In contrast to his wife's bath, Craig's is more deliberately done up. "He wanted a fabulous showpiece," says Siskin. "Craig is open to new ideas, and if he likes something, he'll go for it. He doesn't beat himself up about whether it's completely practical." Siskin gave his client dapper walls striped with bold horizontal bands of limestone and beige marble. "I'd seen that banding detail somewhere—I can't even remember where—and loved it," he says. The chic stripes play off exotic accents like the rosewood vanity, which is actually a repurposed 1960s Danish console. The bowfront armoire in the corner is also rosewood. "Both pieces lend the space a furnished quality," he says. "This looks like a living room, not a bathroom."

Floored in marble mosaic tiles, the room is bisected by a plane of glass that cordons off the shower. "I despise enclosed showers, so I made this one as open as possible,"

Clockwise from above left: Wood-paneled walls and dark-stained wood floors make Diane Soloman's bath feel more like a living room. The pool house sink's ribbonlike wall-mounted faucet plays off the oval-shaped mirror above and is square surface-mounted and peeks out over the edge of the gray-lacquered vanity. Diane Soloman's bathroom is furnished with a console formed from an antique metal armor box; Siskin kept the walls empty so she can install artwork as her collection grows. Above a curvaceous sink is a mirror framed in silver leaf. Antique Danish cabnetry adorns Craig Soloman's bathroom and complements the wall pattern.

says Siskin. "I like the idea of a bathing *room*—a room that's one big shower. If I could, I'd just put a big drain in the center of the room and call it a day."

This shower is perhaps the closest Siskin has gotten to fulfilling his own dream. "Craig embraced the concept, since he has a small shower at home in the city. And he didn't need a sealed-off shower for steam, because there's a steam room downstairs for the whole family." What his client did want was a variety of showering options, including handheld, rainfall, and wall-mounted fixtures. "Multiple showerheads is a big trend today. I think it's because the shower is one of the few places in the home for masculine self-indulgence," says Siskin.

In front of the shower window is an ornamental stone console designed for the outdoors. It's used for soap and shampoos, as well as a pedestal for plants and artwork like his rooster sculpture.

Down the hill from the main residence is the pool house, the main locus of family entertaining. At one end is a stucco-clad enclosure housing the laundry area and the bath, which doubles as a changing room for guests to slip in and out of bathing suits. One corner is overtaken by a walk-in shower with glass doors and brushed-nickel hardware that's minimalist to the extreme. All four walls are clad in rectangular porcelain tiles, reflecting Siskin's yen for geometry. The vanity wall is an artful interplay of different shapes: an oval mirror and a rectangular shelf are juxtaposed with a skinny linear faucet and the gray-lacquered vanity's square sink. "The design here is really more about having fun. A pool house isn't used on a daily basis, so you don't have to be so careful about the functional requirements."

That sentiment sums up the mood of the entire property. "We have the same laid-back sensibility here that we had in the old teardown, yet with a much more luxurious and lasting design," says Soloman. She credits Siskin for creating a spacious home that's at once private and public—and also quite personal. "By designing with a sense of humor and with our particular lifestyle in mind, he created a home that's light and free and puts the focus on quality time together with loved ones."

Opposite: Diane Soloman's soaking tub is more of a sculptural centerpiece than a frequently used feature. "I thought I might use it but I haven't yet," she says, laughing.

modern boudoirs

The strict definition of a boudoir is a woman's private retreat. In eighteenth-century France, when these feminine sanctuaries first became fashionable, they were more an extension of the bedroom than the bath.

During a time when men and women occupied separate spheres (both in society and in the home), this was a room from which a lady conducted her affairs—at that time, managing the domestic sphere.

But over the centuries, as the female's role in society has evolved from homemaker to career woman, the boudoir took an introspective turn, morphing into an inner sanctum, a place to retreat from the world rather than engage with it. And while the boudoir was once an adjunct to the bathroom, now the boudoir *is* the bathroom— albeit furnished more like a living area than a utilitarian, function-first space. Today, a woman's sanctuary may very well reference the classical styling of its predecessors, but those wood-paneled walls and cozy lounges are just a few feet away from the plumbing fixtures.

For the pied-à-terre of a New York jet-setter, architect Joan Chan designed a dressing and bathing area modeled on a 1930s boudoir by Adolph Loos. The owner enjoys a large dressing room, separate bathing area, and her own private terrace—as well as glamorous, light-catching finishes and resplendent pink onyx walls that infuse her space with old-world glamour. Every detail works in concert to help her recharge and relax. Where the boudoir was once a buffer between the bedroom and the more public areas of the home, now it's the most secluded spot in the house—which, to the modern woman, is often a great luxury.

Today's boudoirs often represent a more liberal interpretation of the term, with spaces that aren't necessarily private—and not just for ladies, but still very much a sanctuary. For a Manhattan couple, Peter Balsam designed an extravagant space

Previous pages: Joan Chan installed a pair of antique glass doors etched with strutting peacocks to separate her client's vanity and bath.

oriented around hypnotic materials—red onyx, rock crystal—countered by high-tech gadgetry like a programmable lighting system (for him) and an LED-lit soaking tub (for her). While busy couples often dream of sharing the space, in reality they are often not home together. So, ultimately, a supposedly "shared" space might be used by each spouse at different times of the day—eliminating the need for separate his-and-hers spaces.

In her 1902 treatise *Decoration of Houses*, novelist and design authority Edith Wharton encouraged women to appoint their drawing rooms with an eye to simplicity, judiciously furnished with objects of contemplation that they would not grow tired of seeing every day. In suburban New Jersey, the CEO of a luxury stone and tile company took those words to heart, treating herself to a bathing oasis imagined by architecture firm Babey Moulton Jue & Booth. With a warehouse of exotic stones and surfacing materials—Calacatta Gold and Breccia Imperiale marbles, sable onyx, Blacklip seashell inlay—at her disposal, the client masterminded a dazzling design that channels diverse inspirations, from high-end hotels to historic glass artisans. What's distinctive and relevant is that the space was designed around one of the owner's most prized possessions: a rare 1930s Lalique crystal chandelier, an object that would normally have pride of place in the living room, where she could show it off to others. But instead, it's installed where *she* can see it most often, and where she is most relaxed and centered.

Contemporary boudoirs are often shared with a significant other—or sometimes an entire family. Designer and girl-about-town Celerie Kemble has a master bath that also services her husband, son, and two pets. The tasteful 1920s-style refuge doubles as her walk-in closet, thanks to a voluminous antique armoire housing her Chanel and Christian Louboutins, which overtake a majority of the space. For the young mom and urban professional, the concept of a boudoir isn't about full-time privacy and pampering. It's about knowing when to shoo everyone out on occasion so she can indulge in a languorous, refreshing solo soak after a long workday. What could be more modern?

a stone's throw
from pompeii

"I WAS EXTREMELY ATTACHED TO MY OLD BATHROOM," says Rose Caiola, describing a classical Italian design with walls of dramatic gold-flecked marble. But after having two kids, she and her husband, Carl, had outgrown their Upper East Side home and were expanding into the neighboring apartment. Reworking the space meant building an entirely new master suite—bath included.

The couple called their interior designer, Peter Balsam, with whom they've collaborated for seven years. Husband and wife, who both work in real estate, spend a lot of time looking for unusual building materials and finishes. Together, Caiola and Balsam scoured almost every bath showroom in New York. Everything clicked one day at a tile emporium, where a mosaic floor medallion caught her eye. The design, inspired by a fifteenth-century Italian motif, featured a simple but sophisticated pattern of arabesques arrayed like an eight-point compass. "When I get something in my head, it's hard to dissuade me," she says, laughing.

For the walls, they wanted a stone that would match the floor medallion in both coloration and pizzazz. A friend of Caiola's who owned a marble yard encouraged her to consider red onyx. "He said, 'It's really different, very unusual, and we don't get it very often.' When I saw it, I said, 'Wow!'" Sliced through with rivers of crystal, it's no shy wallflower.

The stone's animated pattern, however, proved tricky to design around. Balsam confesses, "After we picked out all the slabs, I spent a lot of time using computer-aided drawing programs to determine how the pieces should be placed. With stone this busy, you have to treat the slabs like paintings."

The resulting room recalls an opulent, old-world Pompeian bath. The floor medallion, customized in reddish shades of marble, has pride of place in the vanity area, lit

Previous pages, left: Rose and Carl Caiola's bathroom is surfaced in dramatic red onyx. It took six slabs to cover the entire bathroom. Peter Balsam designed the room around the specific figuration of each onyx slab so they would complement one another. Previous pages, right: The toilet and bidet room is tucked behind a sliding glass pocket door etched with a flowering cherry blossom motif for privacy. Crystal wall sconces create a subdued glow within. Opposite: The back of the bathroom steps up to a two-person soaking tub, outfitted with air jets and an LED lighting system that can be programmed to change color. Elaborate carved arches surround three walls of the soaking area to accommodate accessories and candles.

by a crystal chandelier. To the left, behind a frosted-glass door etched with flowering cherry blossoms, is a separate room for the toilet and bidet. Off to the right, a hallway leads to a glassed-in shower equipped with numerous water sprays, as well as a body bar, rain showerhead, and steam unit. A transom window flips open to let steam escape.

Beyond the shower is an elevated soaking tub filled by faucets with rock-crystal handles. Balsam used the crystal-accented hardware everywhere, from drawer pulls to the shower controls. "They are like pieces of jewelry, beautifully accentuating the striations in the onyx," he says.

Lights recessed in the ceiling coves above the tub and vanity bathe the marble in a warm glow. "Every corner of the room is lit separately and attached to a dimmer," says Balsam. "Carl likes to mix things up and create different lighting effects. He is so savvy about that technology." So, apparently, are the kids. "They always turn up the colored LED lights in the tub and then shut off all the overheads," says Caiola.

She explains that the soaking tub, enveloped in three walls of onyx, is the best spot from which to enjoy the stone. "Shapes start to present themselves in the veins—animals and people, for instance," she says. "Just two nights ago, while taking a bath, I saw the profile of a woman with her hand under her chin. You see something new every time you look at it."

On each wall, Balsam created arched nooks to hold candles and decorative objects. Such details proved particularly difficult to fabricate in onyx, he says. "We had to make samples of everything to see if the stone could work in the profiles we chose." Balsam had an expert collaborator in Carl, who worked closely to design every arch. "My husband is meticulous," says Caiola. "Without him, this project would have never happened. I'm not a detail person. There's so much involved in this kind of design. It takes five heads, twenty discussions, and at least as many samples." But, she adds, it's worth it in the end. "Then you get to fall in love all over again—with a new space."

Opposite, clockwise from above left: Hardware throughout is rock crystal with polished-nickel details. The steam-shower controls are within arm's reach of a built-in bench. Faux-aged mirrors above the sinks are a contemporary design. The eight-pointed floor medallion near the vanity was the first element that Rose Caiola decided on. She had a custom version made in four varieties of marble to match the surrounding onyx.

bathing beauty

DESIGNER CELERIE KEMBLE LEADS A GLAMOROUS DOUBLE LIFE. By day, she's all business: a young urban mom with a hectic schedule and a high-profile New York job designing furnishings for big-time manufacturers and houses for boldfaced names. But by night, this girl-about-town slips on a Chloé blouse and sexy Christian Louboutin stilettos en route to the hottest downtown boîtes.

Tucked into a hallway between the kitchen and the master bedroom, Kemble's handsome boudoir reflects her work-hard, play-hard lifestyle. The space is about function *and* pampering. With a wraparound armoire for stashing clothes, the chic black-and-white bath conveniently doubles as her dressing room: she can shower, dress, apply makeup, and even feed her beloved Jack Russell terrier, Anchovie, all within a few feet. "It's mission control for the whole house," she says.

Yet there is nothing utilitarian about the space. A gamine side chair upholstered in white terry encourages lounging. The Thassos marble vanity poses on come-hither crystal legs. "Crystal is graceful and ethereal—the legs seem almost liquid," Kemble explains. And the wraparound armoire is lined in luxurious powder blue faux leather and filled with to-die-for couture. The heavily carved piece is actually an antique French apothecary cabinet, bought at one of Kemble's favorite shops. "It's from 145 Antiques in New York. I fell in love with the dark, old wood, probably ebonized mahogany, and its turn-of-the-century look." Kemble used the piece for many years to store toiletries and towels. "But then I met my husband and moved in with him— and was in desperate need of a closet."

She sent the piece to her local cabinetmaker to be converted into an armoire. He made it deep enough for hanging clothes by adding a few inches of matching wood to both sides; Kemble chose the Lucite clothes rod to play off the vanity's crystal legs.

Previous pages, left: The L-shaped armoire—Kemble's closet—is actually two separate pieces. The one on the right is antique; the piece on the left was built by her cabinetmaker to match. "The original was only about sixteen inches deep, so he cut out the back and deepened it to make it big enough for clothing," she explains. Previous pages, right: Kemble purchased the marble soaking tub in Argentina and had it shipped to New York. "It's from an early-twentieth-century hotel, so it matches the look of the space." A framed 1950s map of New York City hangs above. Opposite: Located at the crossroads of designer Celerie Kemble's bedroom, her son's room, and the kitchen, this bathroom sees a lot of hustle and bustle. Even the family pets, Anchovie and Opossum, have their own space below the marble vanity.

She also had her cabinetmaker widen the piece, adding drawers and adjustable shelves to store her jewelry and creams. "The expansion was a desperate attempt to create more storage," she says, laughing. "I am a hoarder! I'm constantly in flea markets buying vintage jewelry and accessories."

Kemble's attachment to a certain kind of fashion—vintage-inspired, a bit architectural—is reflected here. "If you look at my wardrobe, there's nothing flouncy. I'm not a girlie girl. So I didn't want a feminine bathroom," she says. "The design was really more about channeling an industrial, old New York look." Hence the schoolhouse-style pendant lights, black-and-white basket-weave floor tiles, and neutral hues. "When it comes to bathrooms, I like clean lines and just one or two colors. Because there is so much action in this one room, I used every trick to keep it soothing."

Kemble gabs on the phone with her mom—also an interior designer—from the comfort of her antique marble soaking tub. She had the piece shipped from Argentina: "I found it through a salvage shop. From the photos, it looked promising enough to risk sending it thousands of miles. But it was tied up in customs for months." She was relieved that the tub ended up being as divine as she had hoped. "I love the clean lines. And because it was from a 1920s hotel, it fits right in with the room's period look." A framed 1950s map of New York City hangs above. "It's fun to look at the scale of the buildings from the safety of my warm little tub. When I'm alone in there, I feel a peacefulness that I find nowhere else in my life."

Indeed, most of the time, the room is a full-family gathering spot. "My husband thinks of it as his space," she jokes. "It's also not unusual to find the dog, baby, and husband all in the tub at once. Opossum sits on the lounge chair and watches. She hates the water—but she also hates to be left out of anything."

And so do Kemble's pals: "Whenever I have parties, I wind up in my sanctuary gossiping with three or four friends. I'll need a little break from the crowd and go hide out there; only my close friends know where to find me. We jokingly refer to it as the VIP lounge."

Opposite, clockwise from above left: Above the toilet is framed artwork made from black vintage buttons, which mimic the wallpaper's circular graphic. The floor is tiled in black-and-white basket-weave-patterned ceramic. The vanity's slab of Thassos marble floats on clear crystal legs. The walls are clad in 18-inch Carrara marble tiles, installed with a super-tight grout line so that it looks like slabs. The restrained color palette instills a sense of turn-of-the-century New York glamour. Kemble's bathroom boasts a large walk-in shower. Taps over the hammered-nickel sink are mounted to the wall, freeing up the surface area below.

age of opulence

AS FOUNDER AND CEO OF A LUXURY STONE AND TILE COMPANY, Nancy Epstein spends the majority of her days scouring the globe in obsessive pursuit of rare marble, exotic onyx, and other precious surfaces. During any given week, she might trek to a remote European quarry to hunt down a few coveted slabs of near-extinct stone, or drop by an artist's studio in the glassblowing mecca of Murano, Italy. Her journeys mix business and pleasure: while sourcing merchandise for her company, Artistic Tile, she often has the opportunity to indulge her related passion for art glass, a fondness she shares with her husband, Larry. "We've been collecting works by Lalique, Tiffany, and other legends for more than two decades," says Epstein. "To me, what makes these designs so special is that each object is formed by the artisan's own hands and breath," she says. "Such an intensely physical process results in incredibly ephemeral pieces. And no two are exactly alike."

During their travels, the two have become equally avid connoisseurs of another design genre: luxury hotel interiors. No surprise then that they were thrilled to discover that two of their favorites places to stay—Chicago's Peninsula Hotel and the Villa Feltrinelli on Italy's Lake Garda—were designed by the same architectural firm: Babey Moulton Jue & Booth. They immediately called the company's San Francisco office and asked them to redesign the master suite of their suburban New Jersey home.

The firm's Pamela Babey and Alan Deal created an ornate Art Deco–style boudoir to showcase their clients' many passions. Highlights from the Epsteins' art-glass collection are displayed against an almost unfathomable array of opulent finishes, from manta-ray skins to iridescent shell inlay. The layout of the space was even inspired by Nancy's most prized possessions: a pair of 1930s Lalique chandeliers—one a pool of

Previous pages, left: The 1930s Lalique chandelier in the octagonal rotunda sparked the design of the entire master bath. Skylights above are screened with a pattern of steel circles that echo the geometry of the room. Running throughout the floor of the master suite is Calacatta Gold marble mosaic installed in a classical Italian pattern. Sable onyx ribbons are inlaid in the honey-toned marble mosaic floor. Arched doors of Breccia Imperiale marble encircling the perimeter of the bathing rotunda lead to walk-in closets and his-and-hers WCs. The rotunda walls are clad in antiqued mirror handmade by an artisan based in Murano, Italy. Previous pages, right: Passageways between the octagonal rotundas are inlaid with Blacklip seashell. Recesses in the shell-inlaid walls accommodate the bedroom door's cobalt-glass knobs. Opposite: Doors leading to the master bedroom have screens patterned with steel circles, which mimic the rotunda skylights.

glowing orbs, the other a dramatic showstopper with eight radiating cut-glass fins. "I'd waited more than a dozen years to buy that chandelier," says Epstein. "The piece was made in a very limited edition, and they don't come to the market very often. I wanted my rare find to be the centerpiece of the design."

And so it is. Taking cues from the eight-sided fixture, the architects designed a suite of back-to-back octagonal rooms. A passageway inlaid with Blacklip seashell leads from the master bedroom to the smaller of the two octagons, which serves as the dressing area. Paneled in African sapele wood, the intimate vestibule has doors on both sides opening onto his-and-hers closets. Built-in dresser drawers recessed into four of the room's walls have niches to display colorful glass vases and statuettes. "Just walking into this room transports me to Venice, watching glassblowers at their craft," says Epstein. "I love being surrounded by all the things that I adore during my little bit of private quiet time each morning."

Flowing through the entire master suite is a sinuous mosaic floor of honey-toned Calacatta Gold marble. The wavelike pattern draws the eye in to the octagonal main bathing area, where it's inlaid, like a precious gift, with ribbons of auburn-hued sable onyx. "The loop-de-loop motif was modeled on the metalwork of a staircase I saw in Brussels, designed by Art Deco architect Victor Horta," Epstein explains. The soaring rotunda is capped by skylights screened in clusters of steel circles, which echo the room's bold geometries. Suspended below is the pièce de résistance: the glittering Lalique chandelier, reflected ad infinitum in the mirrored rotunda walls. "I really wanted to use antiqued mirror but was worried that I would just see myself everywhere—and one thing I can't stand is a mirrored bath," says Epstein. "Alan and Pamela assured me that the antiquing would obscure reflections."

On either side of the rotunda are separate his-and-hers vanities, topped with silvery slabs of the same Breccia Imperiale marble used for the backsplash and surrounding archways. The incredibly rare stone is one of Nancy's favorites. Because the marble occurs so close to the earth's surface, it was quarried first; the last slabs were removed from the ground more than a century

Opposite, clockwise from above left: A globe-style antique Lalique chandelier lights the dressing vestibule. Larry's WC is equipped with a flat-screen TV for watching the morning news. Inspired by a similar piece that Nancy happened upon in a Venice fashion boutique, vanity legs are stacked with glass balls of varying colors and size, including clear bubble glass and a lipstick-red orb. The shower is tiled in pale green glass stick mosaics installed in an ashlar pattern; for added dimension and texture, the architects alternated satin and gloss finishes.

ago. After years of hounding her contacts, Nancy turned up a few blocks, which had been left languishing at the edge of a remote Italian quarry. "It always drove me crazy that Americans had no access to the elaborately veined marbles you see everywhere in Europe—and that are the grace notes of so many of the historic places we love to visit when we go abroad."

Below the marble countertop, vanity drawers are surfaced in creamy ivory shagreen. The detail was inspired by 1970s designer Karl Springer, who made liberal use of the manta-ray skins in his elegant Deco-style furnishings. "I wanted shagreen somewhere, so Alan put it front and center on my vanity, where I'd see it every day," says Epstein. Legs of polished nickel are strung with hand-blown glass balls in varying sizes and finishes. Groupings of similar glass orbs form effervescent light fixtures above, which burst from the wall like champagne bubbles.

The sinks are also glass, hand-etched with delicate stripes. At night, they glow from beneath. Indeed, night lighting is a major feature of the suite's design. Recessed below the marble mosaic floors are motion-sensitive fiber-optic pathways leading from both sides of the bed to the his-and-hers water closets off the main rotunda. The suite even has remote-controlled bidet-style toilets, with motion-activated lid lifters and seat heaters operated from wall-mounted touch pads in the WCs. Such well-considered features make the room as user-friendly as it is lavish.

Surrounded by all her life's passions, Nancy is nonetheless able to list her favorite aspect of the design: the chance to meet one of her glassblowing idols. Visiting the Venice studio of an artisan producing antiqued glass for the rotunda walls, she encountered a bit of a language barrier. The artist called his bilingual neighbor over to translate. "I almost fainted when I realized that our 'interpreter' was none other than *the* Lino Tagliapietra, a renowned studio-glass artist whose work is in museums everywhere," she says, still giddy at the thought. Of course, the experience only left her wanting more: "Now if only I could go back in time and meet René Lalique and Louis Comfort Tiffany, too."

Opposite: The vanities are topped with the same rare Breccia Imperiale marble used for the backsplash and the rotunda's arched doorways. The drawers below, which pivot to each side, are surfaced in ivory shagreen. The vanities are lit by exuberant bubble-glass fixtures, handmade in France. Art Deco–style polished nickel faucets were chosen to match the vanity legs.

light and lively

JOAN CHAN'S LUMINOUS DESIGN for an Upper East Side boudoir shows off the transformative power of architecture. "No matter what your frame of mind before you open the door, once inside you can't help but feel like a movie star," she says. It could be the dazzling finishes like mother-of-pearl and pink onyx, which lend a heady dose of cinematic glamour. Or the private terrace with formal gardens and twentieth-floor views of Central Park. Or, perhaps, the diffused daylight, which bounces off mirrored walls to immerse visitors in a lustrous haze of illumination. The effect is not unlike that of a classic Hollywood film, in which starlets were painstakingly lit from every angle so they'd look their dewy best—no matter what narrative chaos was unfolding around them. Courtesy of the soft glow and warm, flattering hues, the architect's soigné design ensures that her client—a former model who's spent her fair share of time in front of the camera—is always ready for her close-up.

While the rest of her home was designed for entertaining, the resplendent boudoir is the client's private sanctuary. The room is off-limits even to her husband, who has his own bath at the other end of the master suite. Situated on the north side of the sun-drenched apartment, the boudoir is awash in ambient light throughout the day. "The space is all about views and reflections," says Chan. "My idea was to make it a prismatic jewel box, reflecting inward and outward." She placed the dressing area along the window wall so her client could take advantage of natural light. On either side of the window are floor-to-ceiling closets. Their doors are mirrored to reflect the view; from certain angles, the walls appear to melt away and the room becomes an extension of the outdoors.

Chan avoided elaborate details in favor of feminine but unfussy flourishes like the rippled moldings framing the mirrors. She modeled the detail on a 1930s dressing

Previous pages, left: Architect Joan Chan considered quartz and marble for the bathing area, but settled on pink onyx both for its translucency and its skin-enhancing effect. A low storage unit housing drawers for clothing divides the dressing area in two. The counter is topped with shimmering, light-catching mother-of-pearl tiles. Previous pages, right: The central storage unit steps down at one end to form a curved vanity table. Inspired by the technique used by Frank Lloyd Wright at Fallingwater, Chan de-silvered the circular mirror's rim and installed recessed lights behind. Opposite: The gilded toilet-paper holder is recessed into the wall for a cleaner look. Jewel-like gold-finished hardware and bath accessories are detailed with rock crystals. Pink onyx is accented with bands of pure white Greek Thassos marble, chosen for its lack of veining.

room by Viennese architect Adolph Loos, known for his pared-down, almost rigorous ornamentation. "I discovered the space in a book of Loos's work and was taken by his use of reeded flutings—there was such a lightness to them. And, because it's such a modular element, it could be adapted to fit any space." She selected other embellishments to make sunlight dance around the room: gilded door pulls, crystal chandeliers, gossamer window sheers, and mother-of-pearl tile countertops surfacing the central storage unit and the built-in vanity table. The bright space shimmers all the more in contrast to dark chocolate wengé floorboards.

Chan oriented the vanity mirror facing away from the window so her client is lit head-on when applying makeup; daylight also bounces in from the full-length mirrors on both sides, creating an even glow that smooths over shadows. For nighttime primping, the mirror is encircled by incandescent strips; Chan de-silvered the outer rim to recess the light source behind.

Behind the vanity, a pair of glass doors etched with strutting peacocks leads into the bath. "The translucent panels create a sort of veiled entrance to her inner sanctum," says Chan, who happened upon the doors at an antiques shop in Lexington, Kentucky. "It was a serendipitous find—peacocks are one of my client's favorite birds."

The bathing area beyond is swathed in slabs of pearlescent pink onyx, which pull light in from the dressing room. "We looked for a semiprecious stone that was regal and had a depth of color," Chan explains. "I knew instinctively that pink onyx would be the most flattering to her skin tone. Chan accented the walls with gold-finished rock-crystal hardware and bands of snow white Greek Thassos marble. "The Greeks are quarrying less and less of it, so it's becoming quite rare," says Chan.

Perhaps the most dramatic part of the boudoir is the private terrace overlooking the city. After a soiree, the lady of the house can remove her jewelry at the vanity, soak in her onyx-clad tub, and repair solo to her terrace. What could be more cinematic, after all, than sitting in the dark surveying the glittering Gotham cityscape—the whole world at her feet?

Opposite, above: Gauzy window sheers in the dressing room create a glowing, gaslight effect, creating privacy while letting in daylight. The existing 5-inch wengé flooring anchors pale, luminous materials like white woodwork and mother-of-pearl counters. **Opposite, below:** Chan used muted colors on the terrace to highlight the foliage and the cityscape beyond.

voyeur

The bathroom's primary function as a place for hygiene and pampering would seem to demand a certain seclusion. But the concept of bathing area as private retreat has been turned, quite literally, inside out.

These days, busy couples and even families spend time together in the bath, treating it as a communal space. More extreme, however, is a trend of voyeuristic spaces that push the concept of visibility to often cheeky extremes: loos wrapped in see-through glass, soaking tubs placed in high-traffic areas, and bathrooms that aren't even rooms, per se, but a loose grouping of wet areas with few or no walls in between. To the uninitiated, these spaces may seem immodest at best and even a bit shocking, challenging, as they do, a prevailing culture of prudishness that's rooted in Victorian times.

But the owners of such extroverted baths don't think of them as voyeuristic. The bathroom may be a charged space, and its associations with cleanliness and private activities still linger. These rooms address practical, even commonplace needs and urges—such as a yearning for spaciousness and views. Designer Mark Nichols dreamed up a spalike Palm Springs retreat that demonstrates one facet of this new openness. There is no enclosure separating the shower from the rest of the space, making the not-so-large room feel much airier while preserving views out to the pool. Placed just inside French doors to the backyard, the bathing area conveniently doubles as a semiprivate outdoor shower—and, thanks to tiled surfaces throughout, the whole room is one big wet space. Nichols admits that the design is a bit sexy. But the space is attuned to its surroundings: exposing bare skin and wearing few clothes are strategies to cope with the hot desert climate.

Laura Bohn, too, communes with nature at her Greenwich Village penthouse, with a tub and shower that peek into a bamboo courtyard. Her vanity, meanwhile, overlooks the city so she can watch foot traffic below—stitching her inner sanctum to the outside world. To many, the bath is not a secluded spot but a place to stay engaged with the world at large; Bohn's flat-screen TV certainly hints at her own such desire.

A wish for views out is often the impetus for building a voyeur bath; views in become the unintended consequence. But in order to connect with the outdoors—whether the desert or the city—people are willing to stretch the boundaries of propriety

Previous pages: In Laura Bohn's bathroom, a wall of floor-to-ceiling glass bordering the bamboo courtyard folds over like a skylight to bring light in from above.

before drawing their curtains. A Miami master bath by architect Alison Spear is an example of such a provocatively public space. For a young family that lives a beachy, indoor-outdoor life, she created a bathroom that's one part breezeway, with a soaking tub that shimmies up against floor-to-ceiling glass—within sight of a boat-trafficked waterway. The couple wanted to see out to the yard and the water; indeed, they bought the property for its views. While they've made some concessions to privacy by installing trees on either side of their yard so the neighbors can't see in, the back remains exposed to the water. The balance between openness and overexposure may lean to the latter, but living in such a space encourages people to shed their inhibitions—and they often find it surprisingly liberating.

For some, the quest for openness is motivated by another reason entirely: to move through space more easily and save time and mental energy in so doing. Architect René González pushes exhibitionism in this direction. Desiring a less compartmentalized, more free-flowing master suite in his Miami Beach apartment, he did away with a separate bathroom altogether. Instead he grouped individual plumbing pods around the periphery of his gallerylike master bedroom: the shower has a door but the toilet does not. Such a configuration seems best suited to singles, perhaps; it works perfectly for González, who tailored the architecture to his own habits and rituals.

An even more experimental example of the voyeur bath is in a New York apartment designed by architect Joel Sanders. Screened in blue glass walls that show shadowy movement behind, the bath glows at the center of the open-plan layout. Sanders has designed a number of similarly subversive spaces that challenge notions of modesty and rethink our need for privacy. But the most revealing aspect of the design is that it's grounded in utilitarian concerns: the placement of the bath next to the kitchen, at the center of the home, and the influx of daylight into a windowless interior room. The layout suggests an interest in rethinking the role and function of the bath completely, and a willingness to let go of outdated conventions that don't support the clients' way of living.

This relaxation of convention gets to the heart of the voyeur bath. While they may seem, at first glance, avant-garde and somewhat conceptual, all embrace a practical—and open-minded—approach to contemporary lifestyles.

a postmodern prewar

REAL ESTATE WISDOM SUGGESTS that when renovating a Manhattan prewar apartment, it makes sense to preserve the old-world proportions and carved moldings characteristic of the period's architecture—if only for resale value. But the design-savvy buyers of a 1930s Upper West Side apartment were more keen to create a modern, usable space that suited their particular needs than to restore outdated architectural details. "We loved the location but not the layout of the apartment," says the husband, a commercial real estate developer. "And the prewar features weren't so special or distinctive to us. We wanted a home that supported our lifestyle as an active, twenty-first-century family with two young kids and that reflected our interest in contemporary design."

The couple's hunt for a forward-thinking architect led to Joel Sanders, known among design insiders for his avant-garde, often voyeuristic interiors with glass-walled bathrooms and other exhibitionist gestures. "When we first started talking, Joel came by to check out the apartment," recalls the client. "He looked at all the moldings, scratched his chin, and asked what I thought of them. I said, 'They don't mean that much to me.' It turned out to be the right answer."

Sanders set about creating an unexpected yet practical design that would streamline the space and support the young family's fluid way of living. "The prewar plan just did not suit their needs," Sanders says. "It was a fairly awkward series of narrow, Victorian rooms with a small kitchen in the back. It made sense to open it up. Giving the kids room to run around was a huge determining factor." His solution was to gut the space completely and place a floating "pod" in the middle to house the kitchen and bathrooms. Bedrooms are grouped together behind the pod, leaving the rest of the floor plan blissfully open—with a 50-foot stretch of windows overlooking the Museum of Natural History. The beauty of the layout is that it carves the apartment into private and public zones while still allowing easy circulation. In fact, the kids can hop on their bikes and ride circles around the pod, which has provided hours of

Previous pages: Daylight filters through the living room's 50-foot-long window wall and into the bathroom so overhead lights aren't needed when it's light outside. The blue glass looks different depending on the time of day, changing from a dark blue to a pale, watery hue. **Opposite:** The blue glass bathroom floats in the middle of the apartment, adjacent to the kitchen to create one central wet zone. A lowered ceiling above the kitchen-bathroom pod gained a few extra inches of headroom to accommodate recessed task lighting and ventilation.

entertainment. "Doing away with dead-end corridors and enclosed rooms lets the kids scoot around more freely," explains Sanders.

The pod's bathroom is wrapped in blue glass panels that take the place of solid walls. "The color of the glass looks different depending on the time of day," says the husband. "At night it glows from inside and creates light for the rest of the apartment." Light isn't the only thing to filter through, however. "It definitely reveals flickers of movement behind," he says. While a bit daring, the glass-box bath is actually a tamer version of a previous one Sanders had designed with clear acid-etched glass, which sold the client on hiring him in the first place. "Joel's thing is about blurring the boundaries between public and private spaces, which I find fascinating," says the client. He and Sanders agreed, however, that that level of openness would not be practical for a young family with a steady parade of visitors. Instead, they settled on a somewhat opaque blue glass that adds a shot of vibrant color and admits light into the windowless bath—while still allowing privacy. It's easy to tell when the room is occupied, but activity within is obscured. "Even so, it can be a bit much for some people," says the client. "A lot of guests will go down the hall to the kids' bathroom, because it has actual walls and doors."

The blue-walled box is, in fact, two loos in one: a master bath and a guest bath. The room has two toilets and two vanity areas, which can be separated via a sliding door. There are also two ways of entering the pod: one through a pivot door leading from the master bedroom, the other from the living area. "This kind of multitasking space makes so much more sense than having a dedicated guest bath that's rarely used," says Sanders. Indeed, adds the client, "Joel is a genius at creating flexible spaces. It's such a smart use of square footage. I love that you can be in the bathroom at night and feel like you're part of the master suite, and then close two doors and throughout the day it's part of the living space."

To integrate the bathroom with the surrounding decor—a mix of midcentury modern furnishings and contemporary artwork—Sanders brought in interior designer Andy Goldsborough. "The clients wanted something futuristic and innovative, very of the

Opposite, clockwise from above left: A door slides closed along a ceiling track to separate the bath into two smaller rooms, each with its own toilet. The bathroom floors are poured epoxy, tinted pale blue. This detail shot shows the ceiling of the shower pod, which is painted in a slightly different shade of epoxy paint to create the look of one smooth, continuous surface. The epoxy is tinted a slight turquoise to play off dark-stained floors that run throughout the rest of the space. Blue glass panels separating the bathroom pod from the master bedroom form the back wall of the shower. Minimalist European hardware and fixtures enhance the bathroom's groovy, futuristic vibe.

moment," explains Goldsborough, who consulted on finishes and materials. "It's so freeing to be given carte blanche like that." Walls, floor, and ceiling are surfaced in slick epoxy paint—one of the architect's signature materials—which makes the entire room appear wrapped in a continuous, seamless surface. For variety, Goldsborough chose slightly different but complementary shades of pale, icy blue for each wall. Epoxy gave a silky futuristic look, one that meets the clients' desire for a forward-thinking space that's also practical for a young family. The resin-based product—essentially a thin layer of plastic—can be poured on floors for a continuous surface that's waterproof, dirt resistant, and durable, too. It provides the seamless look of concrete but has a slicker, more "artificial" appearance that designers love. It's also a great alterative to tile or linoleum, offering the same wide range of colors but with a grout-free surface that holds up to water. Goldsborough often chooses epoxy for its expressiveness: the material can be customized in a range of colors or embedded with particles like quartz that enhance reflectivity. Epoxy can even be applied like paint to vertical surfaces, as done here, to create the effect of a protective coating that wraps up the floors and on to the walls. Best yet, the groovy-looking material stands up to the wear-and-tear of young kids.

Cabinets are rich walnut with satin-finished stainless-steel accents, chosen to match the dark wood floors running through the rest of the house. Goldsborough selected matte Corian countertops the color of melted vanilla ice cream—sleek but still tactile. Sinks are built directly into the Corian surface so they're easier to clean. "Andy's color and material choices gave this space, which could have veered a little too sleek, a real sense of warmth," says the client.

While the design is imminently functional, it's proven inspirational, too. "Our kids have become attuned to design," says the client. "Whenever we travel, they'll point out details of the hotel room and how the space works, for instance. I think living in a house like this has inspired them to become architects when they grow up." Devout modernists, that is.

Opposite: The walnut vanity is surfaced in seamless white Corian with built-in sinks. The faucets are mounted to the mirrored wall behind for a clean effect.

making a splash

"THIS BATHROOM IS ALL ABOUT COOLING OFF," says designer Mark Nichols. "In Palm Springs, you are constantly exposed to the sun and the elements. I designed this space as an escape from the heat." The soothing space, the master bath of a desert getaway, features glassy, cool-to-the-touch materials in a chilled-out palette of aqua and cerulean. "We tried to create a relaxing, modernist retreat in a very extreme environment," he says.

The ocean blue room is also green. Nichols designed the master bath for a luxury spec house by Contempo Homes, a developer of midcentury-style eco-friendly properties. This one was inspired by a popular 1950s floor plan. "It's modeled on the Alexander homes, modernist prefab structures that were marketed to the masses in the area. It was like buying a house from the Sears catalog. At the time, they sold for nineteen thousand dollars. Now the originals go for a million dollars—if you can get your hands on one." Contempo Homes builds slightly enlarged versions of the original Alexanders, updated for the twenty-first century with environmentally savvy features like solar panels, a tankless hot-water heater, a saltwater pool—and eco-chic bathrooms.

Nichols's design embraces nature while keeping some of her harsher elements at bay. "The house has so much glass, especially along the backyard," he explains. "While I wanted to preserve the views out, the sun beats down relentlessly. So I played around with cool color combinations. It was about creating a certain temperature"—one that hovers around 68 degrees. The walls and the ceiling are dipped in icy blue mosaics made from recycled glass bottles, with a rippled texture that tempers their sleekness. "I loved that the tiles had recycled content as well as a nice sense of depth," he says. "I was conscious of choosing eco-friendly finishes that had some sex appeal. From afar, everything looks rather sleek. But up close, each surface has a strong personality and nuance."

Previous pages, left: No partition separates the shower from the rest of the room. "I've found that more clients are asking for large, open bathrooms," says Nichols. "I'll often mark transitions from wet areas to dry with changes in material or level, but this space didn't seem to need it—the room is one big wet area." A clerestory window above the soaking tub offers views of the desert mountains beyond. Because of their placement high up on the wall, just below the roof overhang, clerestory windows are an effective way to admit daylight while providing shading from the sun. Previous pages, right: Surfaced in quartz agglomerate, a detail of the sculptural above-counter sink. Opposite: The quart-agglomerate countertop is made from recycled materials. The fixtures in the house are engineered to save water.

The mosaics draw out subtle blue highlights in the white terrazzo floor. "We were going for a spalike color palette to recall water; out here in the desert, we all associate blue with the pool.

Below a clerestory window offering views of the leafy tops of palm trees is an expansive built-in tub. The angular tub is also terrazzo, tiled in 18-inch gray squares. "In a modern house, you want to keep the variety of materials to a minimum," says Nichols. "And because the tub was such a unique shape and a major component of the bathroom's design, it had to have the same feeling as the floor." The designer's search for a complementary material led him to the terrazzo tiles, a relatively new product that can be used anywhere—even tubs.

Nichols spent as much time on practical considerations like storage. He designed a double vanity with sinks that eat up very little surface area. "Counter space is always at a premium in bathrooms," he says. Below the quartz-agglomerate countertop—also made from recycled materials—are drawers for housing toiletries. The dark run of cabinetry is faced in wengé veneer with slim polished-chrome hand pulls. "Wood is a tough material to use in the desert due to its tendency to crack in the dry air," Nichols cautions. "I'm always careful about letting wood acclimate before installation. Usually I'll let it sit bundled in the house for six weeks."

A room like this is equal parts master bath and pool house. There's a large soaking tub and a walk-in shower, positioned just inside the sliding glass door to the yard. The tricked-out bathing area boasts four showerheads—two on the walls, plus handheld and ceiling-mount versions. (All the fixtures in the house are engineered to save water.)

No door separates the shower from the rest of the room, but an imperceptibly sloped floor angling down to a drain defines the zones. "All the tiled surfaces let the room function as one big wet space," Nichols says. "There's an element of sex to a space like this: out in the desert, it's so hot that you just want to be naked all the time."

What could be more natural?

Opposite: Sliding glass doors connect the shower to the backyard, which has a saltwater pool. The room is equipped with four showerheads, including handheld and rainshower versions, as well as body sprays. The shower floor angles down slightly to a drain in the center of the terrazzo floor. **Following page:** The walls and the ceiling are tiled in ocean blue mosaics—made from recycled glass bottles—installed with matching grout for a uniform look. The bathroom floor is the same white terrazzo that runs throughout the rest of house. It's flecked with small fragments of blue, green, and gray recycled glass. An oversize soaking tub is clad in 18-inch gray terrazzo tiles chosen to match the look of the floor.

The Green Bath

Mark Nichols's sleek Palm Springs bath features a luxurious assortment of earth-friendly materials and environmentally responsible features that save water, energy, and other limited natural resources. Many of the materials incorporate recycled ingredients that divert waste from landfills—from the glass mosaics to the terrazzo floor and quartz-agglomerate counters. Such compelling finishes make the case that green design doesn't have to look crunchy—it can still feel refined and sleek. Finishes manufactured from recycled products are also a great alternative to stones like granite or marble, which deplete natural resources and often require shipment from foreign countries, consuming a significant amount of fossil fuels.

To comply with California building codes—some of the strictest in the nation—Nichols chose plumbing items that conserve water. Low-flow faucets and showerheads, for instance, are engineered to use less water, while emitting just as forceful a spray as standard versions. Toilets here are water-conservation models, too, saving precious gallons with each flush.

While this bathroom is a stellar example of eco-friendly design, there are many other ways to go green, too. Consider motion-activated faucets that turn on and off with a hand sensor to save water (no more leaving the faucet on while brushing teeth). Although such models have long been popular in commercial settings like airports, luxury manufacturers are now designing beautiful versions for the home—in both contemporary and traditional styles. For cabinetry, choose sustainable, renewable materials like quick-growing bamboo or wood that has been responsibly forested rather than clear-cut (look for products certified by the Forest Stewardship Council). For better air quality, cabinetry should be sealed with water-based, chemical-free finishes and walls painted with products that emit few or no volatile organic compounds (i.e., toxins).

For towels—and bathrobes—forget standard cotton, which requires many pesticides and chemicals to produce. Organic cotton is just as soft on the skin, as are textiles made from bamboo fibers and even wood pulp—available in most major department stores.

peekaboo, i see you

"I'M A MASOCHIST," Sebastien Scemla admits. "It seems that I am always in the process of building a new house."

Proving his passion, the serial renovator confesses that he's moved six times in the last seven years. "I never, ever buy a house with the intention of selling it," he says, laughing. "But you just don't know what the future holds." For this creative executive, the future often seems to include a slightly groovier, slightly better situated house just begging to be transformed.

His current pad, which he shares with his wife and daughters, is on a quiet street in Golden Beach, Florida. The 1950s cottage was a bit snug and needed a new master suite. But it had clean lines and a prime location: just a few blocks from the ocean, with a backyard extending to a busy canal behind. "We wanted to stay consistent with the retro Miami Beach look, which is very midcentury mod, but make it a little more clean-lined and contemporary."

His research led to architect Alison Spear, who is well known for designing seriously modern spaces that are nonetheless suited to casual seaside living—and that offer a whiff of nostalgia. "Alison is an old hand at renovatng vintage Miami Beach homes, and such an expert at drawing out their inherent beauty," says Scemla. "Although I love the process of building houses—it's always been a sideline hobby for me—I don't believe in tearing things down. I prefer to work with what's already there." Spear recast the layout to make it more open. Both the bedroom and the adjacent bath over-look the canal and a lap pool. During the day, the glass seems to disappear, making the suite feel like an extension of the yard.

The bathroom unfolds around a freestanding soaking tub pressed—rather exhibitionistically—right up against the glass. The toilet and shower are off to one

Previous pages, left: Opposite the shower's frosted-glass wall is a Zen courtyard filled with river rocks. A clear glass strip at eye level permits a view out. The toilet area and the walk-in shower both have frosted-glass doors so they can be closed off while the rest of the bathroom remains open to the outside. Previous pages, right: White cotton curtains are inset with a clear band at eye level so the owners can enjoy the view even when they need privacy. The freestanding soaking tub has a knockout view of the concrete-grid patio, blue-tiled pool, and busy canal beyond. The flooring is 36-inch glass tiles. Opposite: The vanity's backsplash is a band of transparent glass mosaic, which is also used in and around the shower.

side, behind frosted-glass doors that offer privacy while making the main space look like a spa. "There's even enough open space in here for side-by-side massage tables," notes Scemla.

"Even though I never plan to sell a house when I'm buying it, I always build it for resale," admits Scemla. "My trick is to keep everything clean, timeless—and white. You can't *not* like white." He and his wife are slowly accumulating pieces for the house, including witty, colorful furnishings by contemporary designers like Philippe Starck and Harry Allen. "With white, anything goes."

Materials are stark and a bit futuristic, such as the matte-finished Corian countertop. The floors are tiled with 36-inch squares of white glass. "I was looking for a clean white marble, which is impossible to find," says Scemla. "We also looked at granite, but it had too many specks in it. This is the plainest material out there, and it has a nice thickness to it. Despite the slick finish, it's not slippery underfoot."

Scemla is not as enthusiastic about the clear-glass mosaic he picked for the backsplash and wainscoting. "Clear glass is not very forgiving. You need a really good installer so you don't see the grout behind."

Spear softened the glossy materials with flowing lines: the sinuous vanity, the oval tub, the rounded edges on drawer fronts and mirrors, and globe-shaped pendant lights. She also included peekaboo elements. The shower overlooks a semiprivate pebbled courtyard through a frosted-glass wall, which has a transparent strip near the top to permit the view. The bathing area's glass wall is curtained with white cotton drapes inset with a clear plastic panel at eye level. Mom and Dad can keep a watchful eye on their daughters playing outside and still have privacy. Because the toilet and shower are screened by frosted glass, the curtains can mostly be left open.

And soon they won't need to be closed at all: "I planted a row of trees along both sides of the property so my neighbors can't see in," says Scemla. The boats in back, however, are another story altogether.

Opposite, above and below: A curved vanity, sculpted from white Corian, has integrated sinks on either end so husband and wife have plenty of room. Architect Alison Spear designed cabinet doors with rounded corners to play off the curvaceous lines of the countertop above. Spear installed globe-shaped pendant lights above each of the vanity's rounded-edge mirrors to create a sense of softness in the stark space. Pulling up to the vanity, Philippe Starck's transparent plastic swivel chair continues the theme of clear and see-through materials.

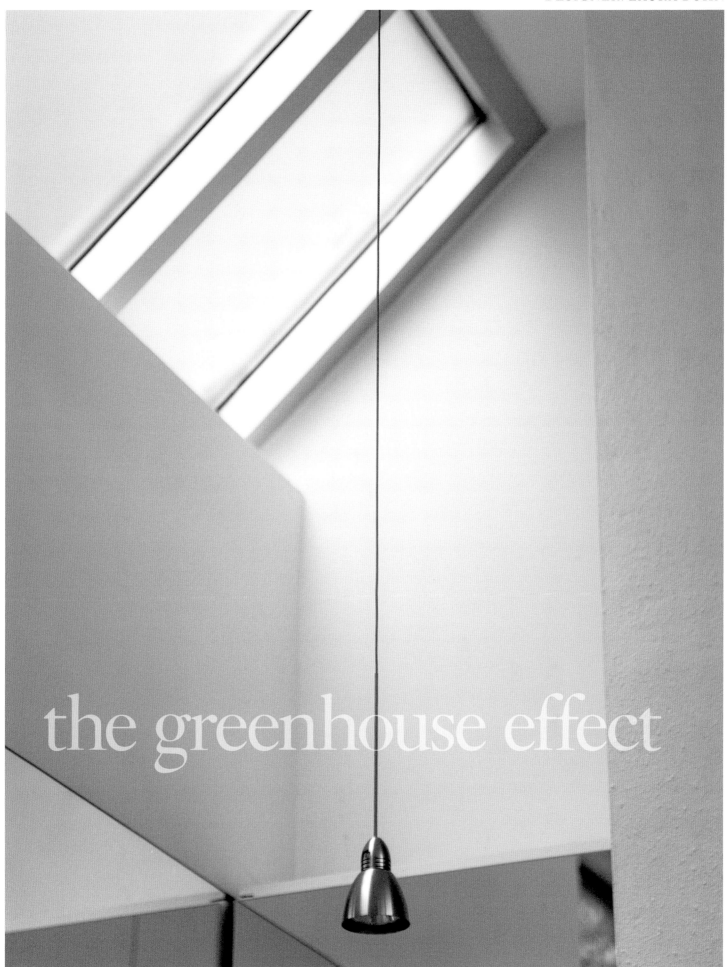

the greenhouse effect

DINNERTIME IS SKETCH TIME for designer Laura Bohn and her builder husband—and sometime collaborator—Richard Fiori. "We could go through a hundred detail drawings during the course of a meal," says Bohn. "We've been to restaurants where they only have cloth napkins and we have to ask for something to sketch on." For this reason, most of their pen-in-hand brainstorming sessions take place in their own apartment, on the second floor of a Beaux Arts–style former bank building in New York. The couple spent four years converting the 1907 landmark into eleven luxury condos, keeping one for themselves. "It was the most complicated thing I have ever designed, but also the most fun," she says.

Their loftlike apartment is surprisingly attuned to the outdoors given its location at the intersection of Fourteenth Street and Eighth Avenue, two high-traffic West Village thoroughfares. In addition to the 600-square-foot grass-covered patio in back, there's a bamboo courtyard that runs through the master suite. Like a greenhouse turned inside out, the courtyard coaxes sunshine into the bedroom and bath on either side—creating a feeling of openness that's usually elusive in the heart of Manhattan.

A tunnel through the bamboo garden bridges bed to bath. Lined with closets, the 13-foot-long tunnel has no windows, making the bathroom feel all the more bright and sun-dappled once you've arrived. The bathroom's back wall, bordering the court-yard, is all glass. Directly across is a large window overlooking the street, with a vanity slipped below. The room is long and narrow—twice as long as it is wide—with a shower on one end and toilets anchoring the other, screened by an aluminum parti-tion. The middle of the room is open, save for a low-slung soaking tub. "We wanted to keep it as airy and expansive as possible in here," says Bohn.

The couple's only other stipulation was his-and-hers sinks. "So I got a big elaborate one, and Richard got a little itty-bitty one," jokes Bohn. "I have a lot of accessories that need to be laid out, while he has a big medicine cabinet and deep drawers for his stuff. A big vanity is totally feminine." Tucked near the door, Fiori's sink is wrapped

Previous pages, left: A wall of floor-to-ceiling glass bordering the bamboo courtyard folds over like a skylight to bring light in from above. Previous pages, right: A slim stainless-steel pendant light illuminates the husband's vanity. Opposite: At one end of the shower is a wheeled newspaper rack, repurposed as a waterproof metal towel bar. The soaking tub's partition wall, surfaced in waterproof Venetian plaster, separates the shower from the rest of the room. The acrylic soaking tub is clad in a sparkly epoxy surface embedded with mirror fragments and marble chips.

in frosted Avonite, creating the effect that it's carved out of ice. His wife's vanity is indeed larger, and no less unusual. It's made from a slatted anodized-aluminum table supporting a shallow, square epoxy sink. "That table is my favorite thing," she says. "I love accessorizing it with plants and lamps. The only problem is that everything falls through the slats." Her original idea was to lay translucent rubber on top, but she never got around to it. "And then I realized that I had adapted: I started to place everything down perpendicularly," Bohn explains.

Below her vanity is a pair of wheeled cabinets made of polished stainless steel. "I bought them from a catalog years ago, and I've taken them with me every time I move," she says. "They weren't even very expensive. But I am a freak about wheels. I love furnishings that can be moved around." Even the shower's metal towel bar— actually a repurposed newspaper rack—has wheels.

Pulling up to Bohn's vanity is a mohair-upholstered armchair from which she can look down onto the street below or watch the news on a TV mounted to the side. The flat-screen swivels so it's viewable from any corner of the room—even from the toilet, which is partially hidden behind the curved aluminum screen. "I'm one of those people who needs to have the TV on at all times," she explains. Yet this is not a room for lounging. "I wanted the space to have a living room feel because that's the kind of environment I like to look at," she says. "But really, who in New York hangs out in their bath-rooms? We certainly don't."

Natural and incandescent lighting play a major role in the design—for both decoration and illumination. The vanity's east-facing window is screened in louvered paper shades that temper the early morning light. "Aside from being beautifully translucent, they are designed to run straight to the top of the window with an almost invisible heading," says Bohn. "As a detail person, I really care about that kind of thing." Suspended in front is an elegant ceiling-hung fixture that casts light up or down as desired. And a stainless-steel pendant dangles artfully over Fiori's sink. "I usually install five or six kinds of lighting in a room so you can switch up the mood," says Bohn.

Opposite, clockwise from above left: The vanity table juts out over the windowsill behind, which is unusually low since the couple raised the floor to accommodate radiant heating below. The floors throughout are diagonally set porcelain tiles, clefted to look like natural slate. The toilet and bidet at one end of the room are screened by a freestanding partition that's aluminum on one side and maple on the other. "I wanted to avoid a rigid wall," Bohn explains. "And it has beautiful connections." Both husband and wife have their own sink and vanity. His is in one corner of the space, clad entirely in Avonite—a nonporous, translucent solid-surfacing product. Bohn repurposed an anodized-aluminum table to use as her vanity. The shallow top-mounted sink is epoxy.

room and board

AT RENÉ GONZÁLEZ'S 1,000-foot modern Miami Beach home, the dividing line between bath and bedroom appears to have washed out to sea. The two are combined in an innovative—and slightly immodest—layout. A glassed-in shower opens onto the sleeping area; a see-through silver curtain is the only nod to propriety. "This is a really great setup for one person," González explains.

Eliminating walls makes the room work almost like a piece of equipment, a series of compartments through which he moves. After his morning shower, he simply grabs his towel, hops out, and is already inside his closet.

The shower, originally a closet, was converted into a wet room. González knocked down a wall in the hallway so he could access the space from his bedroom. Instead of closing it off behind a door, he hung a curtain—the same woven mesh that drapes the toilet area and shower. "The mesh has a sexiness to it," he says. With all three curtains pulled shut, the bathroom and dressing areas are not invisible, exactly, but certainly recede into the background.

The absence of partitions also lets him enjoy his vast contemporary art collection—including works by many fellow Cubans—hung on the walls of his bedroom.

The shower nook is wrapped in gray marble, standard-issue precut windowsills. González oriented the stone vertically and with its rougher back side facing out so it has a bit of grab underfoot.

The out-in-the-open closet demands keeping belongings neat and tidy. It's not a hindrance for González—the kind of design-obsessed individual who would organize his shirts by color and pattern even if they were hidden from view. "Getting rid of closet doors gave me a little more room for clothes," he says, "which is fabulous when you have a small space."

And very few inhibitions.

The toilet, shower, and closet are cordoned off by sheer silver mesh hung from a ceiling track instead of solid walls and doors. González installed fluorescent tube lights behind the track to wash the scrims with light.

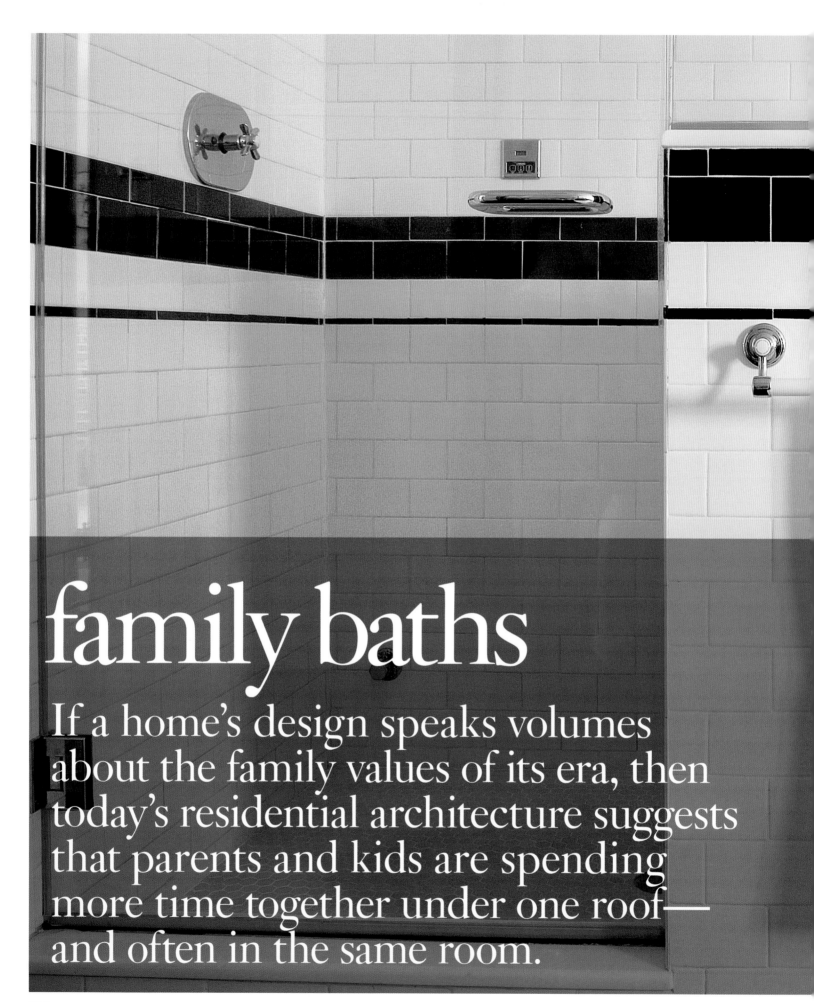

family baths

If a home's design speaks volumes about the family values of its era, then today's residential architecture suggests that parents and kids are spending more time together under one roof—and often in the same room.

Perhaps because couples are older when they start having children and log long hours at the office, they want to be with their families as much as possible. Separate wings are a thing of the past as the entire domicile has become more child focused.

This, of course, means larger living areas and central kitchens. But bath time is often together time, too, and designers are taking note. For a six-year-old girl in New York, Peter Balsam designed a space with a large freestanding tub positioned in the middle of the room so it's easier for Mom or Dad—and often both—to move around when administering baths. More bathrooms are being planned with both child and adult use in mind, which means a comfy perch for parents and a comfy tub for their kids.

The luxury family bathroom isn't, generally, a single space shared full-time by both generations. Indeed, for most, sharing a vanity with a teenage daughter—and her hair accessories and cherry-flavored lip balms—would be a recipe for disaster, not family bonding. Old and young still have their own rooms and ample privacy. But the design of both spaces is beginning to reflect how families choose to spend more time together in both.

Adult bathrooms are becoming more child-friendly, while kids' baths are becoming less youthful. Balsam's design, for instance, strikes a fanciful note, with a decor that speaks to the young client's love of nature and animals via elaborate hand-painted fairy-tale illustrations. But the look is whimsical, not juvenile, with sophisticated colors and finishes for fixed elements like cabinetry and tiles so the room looks otherwise elegant and restrained. Such an aesthetic acknowledges use by a wide age range of occupants—without simply resorting to a neutral look.

Sometimes, parents' and kids' rooms take cues from each other. Designer Michaela Scherrer dreamed up a vintage-chic aesthetic for a California couple with four sons

Previous pages: Tile wainscoting encircles the large walk-in shower equipped with a steam unit designed by Betty Wasserman. The towel bar is set low so it follows the lines of the tile and is accessible for small bathers.

that holds up well to boyish wear and tear. The design of the kids' baths—and the entire house—revolves around used and salvaged sinks, tubs, and toilets revived with a fresh coat of epoxy. Realizing how sturdy, practical, and stylish the shabby-chic design was, the parents requested a similar look in their own bath. These days, there's no longer any hesitation about common tastes that bridge the generation gap. If father and son can share CDs and fashion sensibilities, why not a yen for industrial chic?

Even when master bathrooms are planned as private parental retreats, the spaces seem to get co-opted by the kids. Mom and Dad aren't the only ones who can appreciate the merits of a two-person bathtub embedded with colored lights or a glassed-in shower the size of a small car wash. A design-forward New Jersey couple owns such a place, an adult getaway turned family room. Markus Dochantschi created a loftlike master suite with a glass-enclosed shower floating in the middle. The couple's young kids love to play there—which makes bath time a lot easier for everyone involved. In fact, the family so enjoys spending time together in this space that they use it as a second living room, watching movies together in bed and taking the occasional communal shower (a novelty that will no doubt wear off once the kids, now four and seven, get a little older).

Why not, in such cases, give the kids their own swimming hole–size soaking tub? Most feel there's no need for two in the house, especially when the parents barely have time to use it themselves. Shared elements save square footage and money that could be diverted to other indulgences.

In many cases, a space designed for a solo adult occupant proves that a well-conceived design can function just as expertly when kids come along. Designer, art dealer, and single mom Betty Wasserman built her Hamptons master bath well before she was pregnant with her daughter. But the features that made the room such a great hangout space for adults—spacious proportions, an oversize tub, a plush ottoman, copious storage—have made it just as well suited to its new role as mother-daughter lounge. Of course, her daughter is just five, so Wasserman may have to revisit the design, and even the concept of a shared space, in a few years.

But she can take heart that good design is good design—no matter what age a room's occupant.

WITH FOUR RAMBUNCTIOUS SONS between the ages of seven and thirteen, Elizabeth and David Miller need a kid-friendly home. "I never want to be one of those moms who runs after her kids telling them not to touch things," says Miller. "If something can be broken, it will get broken. For me, it's a luxury to have indestructible stuff. The house belongs to the kids, too, so it shouldn't feel like a museum." The family's Hidden Hills, California, home is the kind of place where floors are beautifully burnished preaged oak and the sofa is slipcovered in a patchwork of French flour sacks. If one section of upholstery gets stained, they can simply stitch another patch on top—a feature that's come in quite handy. "Three hours after the couch was delivered, my youngest, Truman, fell asleep on the sofa with an uncapped Sharpie pen in his hand, and a big black stain spread out across the cushion," she recalls.

The collagelike slipcover and other such well-considered features are the brainchild of interior designer Michaela Scherrer, who also happens to be Elizabeth's cousin. "I was a bridesmaid in her wedding," says Scherrer, who's watched her relative's brood grow steadily. Scherrer's easy-to-maintain, shabby-chic look for the family's home proves that upscale design doesn't have to be pristine and hands-off. "It's still special and luxurious, just in a different way than you'd expect," she says.

In the bathrooms, the decor revolves around vintage furnishings and salvaged fixtures. "I love pieces that already have some nicks and dings," says Scherrer. "Where most people would see signs of age and wear, I see pieces with a backstory, with a sense of history and intrigue. And if one of the kids adds a scuff, it just adds to the life of it." Miller likes the durability of vintage items: "Older pieces are much better designed. The forms are so clean looking and they're much sturdier, too." The cousins spent months scouring salvage yards and swap meets throughout Los Angeles in search of vintage toilets, tubs, and sinks. They even visited buildings slated for demolition, arriving at six one morning to rescue windows from an old commercial loft downtown. "It's harder to find furniture and fixtures this way, but also more

Previous pages: Duncan, Hudson, and Truman's bath has a double sink from an old schoolhouse lavatory. A pair of mirrors framed in bike tires hangs above. Opposite: In Elizabeth and David Miller's master bathroom, the sink counter is galvanized steel, with matching shelves below for towels. The elegant vanity mirror above, detailed with turned brackets, is also vintage. The shallow sink, mounted nearly flush with the countertop for easy cleaning, was bought at a salvage yard. The wall-mounted faucets have a slight curve that lends femininity.

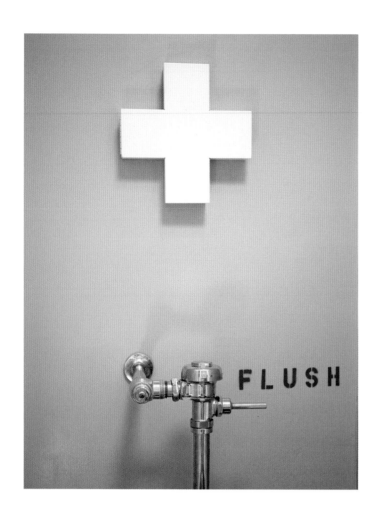

rewarding. You feel like you've really earned each piece," says Scherrer. "The whole process was great fun, and working together made us even closer friends." (Good thing they're both morning people.) Adds Miller, "We concluded that every family with kids—even with all girls—should use salvaged fixtures. It just makes sense."

For the master bath, their treasure hunt turned up a claw-foot tub and a shallow 1940s sink with a surprisingly modern profile. Refurbished with a coat of white epoxy, both are as good as new. The beautiful paint-chipped mirror and armoire are also antique, as are the wire-metal wall hooks and a casement window with graceful curlicue detailing. Even the 1950s light fixtures flanking the sink were salvaged, then updated with glam cut-glass bulbs. The only new items are the countertop and shelves in acid-washed galvanized steel designed to match the lovingly worn aesthetic. "No room is off-limits to the kids—even this one," says Scherrer. "The master bath needed to be just as sturdy as the rest of the house."

All storage is open to keep towels and toiletries accessible. "Elizabeth didn't want a door on anything in the entire house," says Scherrer. "Her lifestyle is grab-and-go." With an eye to future renovations, she also avoided built-in cabinetry in favor of freestanding units. "One of the trickiest parts of the job was adapting to how life progressed," says Scherrer. "Two of the boys who bunked together got to the age where they needed separate rooms. The master bath was originally going to be David's office and might eventually become a closet if they put on an addition. Who wants to spend a lot of money installing a tile floor in a room that could soon become a closet?" The happy result is a space that looks more like a cozy dressing area than a utilitarian bath.

Just across the hallway is the bathroom shared by sons Duncan, Hudson, and Truman. Scherrer lined their shower stall in corrugated metal with fixtures cobbled together from garden valves. "All the fixtures I found in showrooms were so polished that they would have looked ridiculous in the space. And I've always loved the look of these funky knobs, so I had one of my salvage guys make a whole fitting out of industrial pipes." The best part of the system is that users don't have to adjust

Opposite, clockwise from above left: In the children's bathroom, "flush" and "brush your teeth" stenciled throughout are not-so-subtle reminders. A custom storage unit in acid-washed galvanized steel has perforated shelves; "I liked the look of perforation," says Scherrer, "but it took some testing to figure out how big I could make the holes and still have it work as a smooth shelf for knickknacks and bottles." In the shared bathroom, Scherrer designed vintage-style bracket shelves for toiletries. A vintage jewelry hanger keeps Miller's collection of necklaces organized and within easy reach.

the temperature each time they hop in to use the shower; just twist the big red lever to turn the shower on or off. "It's great from an ease-of-use and a safety perspective to prevent scalding," says Scherrer.

Nearby, a pair of rugged tire-frame mirrors hangs above a vintage schoolhouse sink designed for two. In son Jackson's bathroom, she installed a similar lavatory, this one from an industrial laundry facility. "I thought it was very architectural and cool," says Scherrer. Caged school-style lights in both spaces are custom. "It's too hard to get the old ones refitted for contemporary electrical wiring. If I couldn't find the exact vintage item I had in mind—one of the downsides of salvage shopping—we had something new made in a way that didn't feel out of character."

Underfoot are rubber tiles often used for gyms and locker rooms. The boys' bathrooms were originally designed with oak-plank floors like the rest of the house, but Miller replaced them with rubber to hold up better to soggy footprints. "The boys will just hop out of the shower and stand dripping in the middle of the floor," Miller says, laughing. In a vain effort to thwart such boyish behavior, the cousins stenciled phrases on the walls, like "Wash your hands" and "Brush your teeth." It's not just a whimsical detail, Miller explains. "You have to remind boys to do everything! Despite the written instructions, they try to get away with not doing as they're told."

The bathrooms are designed to grow with the boys over time. "I like doing kids' spaces that don't look juvenile," says Scherrer. Nonetheless, the entire house has proved to be more child-friendly than the cousins imagined. "There are tons of kids in this neighborhood, and they all like to hang out here," Miller says with a hint of exhaustion—and more than a little pride.

Opposite: The floors in the master bath and throughout the house are 9-inch planks of preaged oak, finished with an exterior deck stain for added protection. The master bathroom was designed with a minimum of built-ins—the tub is freestanding, as is the shelving—so that it could be easily renovated as the family's spatial needs change. The tub is a salvage-shop find, treated to a new coat of epoxy. "I was drawn to the quirky claw feet, which had a lot of personality," says Scherrer.

storybook bath

ROSE CAIOLA'S heart melts when she reminisces about the first time her daughter saw her new bathroom. "When Sofia Rose walked in there, she went *ballistic*—she absolutely loved it." What six-year-old girl wouldn't be smitten by floors the color of buttercream frosting, a chandelier glittering overhead like a regal tiara, and walls hand-painted with illustrations of bewitching fairies, fluttering butterflies, and roaring lions? "I wanted a design that spoke to my daughter's love of nature and wild animals," she says. "And I couldn't resist the opportunity to do something sweetly feminine—but not infantile."

The whimsical confection is the brainchild of designer Peter Balsam. He says, "A child-friendly space should not look at all childish." Especially for a budding Manhattan sophisticate like Sofia Rose. "The Caiolas are dedicated to exposing their kids to culture," he says, describing a recent mother-daughter trip to Venice to blow Murano glass.

Balsam honed in on a mellow cream color scheme that's warm and enveloping. The designer juiced up the neutral palette with a Venetian mirror framed in gold Murano glass and painted wood cabinets faced with woven cane. The custom mosaic floor is enlivened by abstracted leaves and vines that reiterate the frieze's floral motif.

The centerpiece of the room is a stately bathtub with claw feet. Spacing a tub away from the wall is a boon for parents of small kids, he says. "It allows Mom and Dad full access from every side."

The highlight of the decor is the hand-painting on every surface, like a picture book come to life, by Tim and Andrea Biggs.

The illustrations are scaled to the eyes of a six-year-old; from an adult perspective, the images are actually dainty and rather subtle. And they are easily changed when Sofia Rose—sigh—outgrows them.

Sofia Rose's bathroom is a symphony of creams. The built-in cabinetry is painted with whimsical ribbon and foliage designs. Cream-colored porcelain tiles patterned with a basket-weave motif line the walls. Husband-and-wife artist team Tim and Andrea Biggs hand-painted fairies, birds, ducks, and butterflies on the walls, modeled on a children's storybook. The artists painted a band of roses on the bathtub to mimic the tiled wall frieze. "It really pulled the whole space together," says Balsam.

bubble bath at
the beach

BETTY WASSERMAN DESIGNED HER HAMPTONS GETAWAY well before she was even pregnant with her daughter, Milly. But the chic, easygoing room has turned out to be incredibly well suited to mother-daughter bonding (and pampering) thanks to its airy proportions, ample storage, and a comfortably oversize tub that appeals to bathing beauties of all ages. "It's a room to relax in," says the busy designer and single mom, who also moonlights as a contemporary art consultant. "Whenever I had parties, people would inevitably wind up hanging out here. But these days, my life is more about administering bubble baths to five-year-olds than sipping bubbly—and the space feels just as restful and cozy."

The spacious room is the result of a top-to-bottom renovation. "When I bought the property, a 1930s farmhouse, it was a bit Grey Gardens," she admits, referring to the famously disheveled Hamptons property once owned by Jackie O.'s aunt. "The shrubs looked like they hadn't been trimmed for fifty years, the interiors were dated, and all the rooms were dark. The yard was so overgrown that you couldn't even see out the downstairs windows." And, true to its era, the house had only one bathroom—with no shower!—located on the lower level. "A complete gut was the only option," Wasserman decided.

She blasted open the interiors, combining rooms to make more sweeping, free-flowing spaces. "Big rooms are divine in a weekend home," she says, sighing. Gaining enough square footage to build an upstairs bath required adding a dormer, which proved a bit of a balancing act. "The dormer had to be big enough to accommodate a large bathroom, but small enough to fit the scale of this modestly sized farmhouse. I didn't want it to look disproportionate to the surrounding architecture." She opted to make the windows as large as possible, thus creating the illusion of a smaller structure. The broad expanses of glass also flood daylight inside—a boon during the early-morning hours when Wasserman is up with her daughter.

Previous pages, left: A low white cabinet storing towels near the shower is originally from the kitchen, where it was mounted to the wall by the stove. Wasserman removed it during the renovation and added legs so it could stand on the floor. Previous pages, right: Her daughter, Milly, loves the oversize proportions of the soaking tub. Opposite: White subway-tile wainscoting with a black border adds a note of dapper glamour, which ties into the rest of the home's crisp, modern decor. The bath mat gracing the ebonized floor is a plush nursery rug from the Pottery Barn Kids catalog. "It's like an oversized bath mat, great to lie down on."

The designer wanted the bathroom's interior to mesh seamlessly with the rest of the house, which was reworked into what she calls a country-modern style. "All the rooms are minimal and monochromatic—but still warm and comfortable," she says. "It has the unpretentious quality of a farmhouse, but now the interiors are more streamlined." The bath follows suit. She chose a high-contrast palette of ebonized woods offset by bright white walls and crisp black and white subway tile. The tile wainscoting, which wraps all the way around the room, even the shower, is a throwback to 1930s chic. "Using a tile border is actually quite a switch for me," she says. "It's a bit traditional for my taste, and not something I'd typically do for a client. But it just felt right for this house, which is crisp and clean without feeling slick or contemporary."

Rich ebonized floors balance out the glazed white subway tile. "People think I'm nuts for having a wood floor in the bath, but I like warmth underfoot—and I've never been much of a slipper person," she says. A pair of custom cherry vanities—one for the sink, one for applying makeup—was stained to match the dark floor. "Wood is near and dear to my heart because its organic quality softens the modern lines. I wanted to use as much of it as I could to make the room feel inviting and furnished rather than like it's filled with plumbing fixtures," she explains.

For additional storage, the designer installed a mirrored medicine cabinet above the sink and, beside it, a low-slung glass-fronted unit for towels. The cabinet was salvaged during the kitchen renovation; it once hung on the wall near the stove. "I added legs and sat it on the floor, and presto—a cool cabinet for towels!" And at just the right height for a five-year-old to boot. The copious storage is one of Wasserman's favorite aspects of the design, with ample room for both their belongings. "I love never having to think about where I'm going to store all my bottles and products," she says.

In fact, the urge to maximize storage inspired Wasserman to install just one sink instead of the expected two. "Several friends rather strongly suggested a double vanity for both resale and practicality. But I'm so happy with the resulting design, because it maximizes counter

Opposite: Wasserman opted for a single sink to maximize counter space for her toiletries, artwork, and family photographs.

space." In addition to housing moisturizers and perfume bottles, the countertops are used by Wasserman to display works by some of the contemporary artists she represents, as well as groupings of family photos.

At the far end of the room is a tub big enough for two. "But usually it becomes Milly's indoor swimming pool. She'll climb in after the beach with all her toys. She especially loves drawing on a huge whiteboard with her soap crayons and then wiping it down with her ducky sponge." (A budding art consultant, perhaps?) The designer can pull over the upholstered ottoman from the vanity to administer a rinse with the handheld shower-head. "It's a cozy spot to hang out while she splashes around." Indeed, Wasserman loves the leisurely pace here, where bath time equals playtime. "The beauty of a weekend home is that, other than my morning tennis date, no one has to get out the door at a specific time. Mornings here are nothing like back in the city, where I have to get Milly ready for school every day." (Of course, she's still up early, so window shutters control the influx of daylight. "It's fierce from seven to eight a.m. I adjust them to cast light up on the ceiling, so sunlight doesn't blast in when I'm barely awake.")

In addition to the soaking tub, there's also a steam shower that's great for sharing. "It's so nice to have steam when Milly has a cold." Wasserman also included another feature for more grown-up self-indulgence: "I made sure the room was large enough to fit a massage table—I keep one in each of my homes," she says. "It's easy to have the therapist come over, open up the table, light the candles, and give a massage. I'll take a steam and voilà: instant spa room. I never have to go far to be pampered."

Opposite: Across from the sink is a separate vanity for applying makeup, with an upholstered ottoman that can be pulled over to the soaking tub for administering baths.

all together now

"WE DESIGNED THIS TO BE AN ADULT GETAWAY," says Elizabeth Kubany of the loftlike master bedroom she shares with her husband, Mordechai. "But the reality is that our kids, Benjamin and Lily, are up here all the time. It has basically become a second family room." The space, formerly the Kubanys' attic, looks like an adult lounge: all clean lines, rich materials—and a revealing glassed-in shower floating in the middle. But this sophisticated suite is proof that a grown-up space can be child-friendly, too.

The attic was one of the last parts of the 1930s suburban New Jersey home that the couple renovated. "Because the top floor is so removed from the rest of the house, the redesign felt like an opportunity to do something really different, even radical," says Kubany. She and her husband—an architectural publicist and an insurance executive, respectively—did want to keep certain architectural details like the high-pitched roof untouched, however. "We didn't want to lose that expansiveness."

The couple's architect, Markus Dochantschi of studioMDA, devised an innovative free-flowing layout to retain the room's lofty feel. "The room is forty-five feet long but has only two windows, one at either end," he says. "If you chop up that kind of space, with limited daylight and those sloping eaves, it will always feel like an attic—and not a master suite. I said to Elizabeth and Mordechai, if you're interested in a hybrid design that combines bed and bath into one, I think we can do something amazing here."

His scheme placed the bedroom at one end of the attic and the toilet on the other, with the sink and shower floating in between. The sleeping and bathing areas flow into each other, separated by a plane of clear glass that stretches along the oversize shower. (A hidden pocket door pulls out from behind the shower's back wall to screen the toilet.) A change in flooring height and material—from walnut-stained oak to limestone—is the only other design element that divides the two functions.

Dochantschi turned leftover space below the attic's sloping eaves into a wall of storage, grouping closets and drawers behind a run of white-stained wood doors. The storage

Previous pages, left: Designed by Markus Dochantschi, the master suite takes over the attic of Elizabeth and Mordechai Kubany's 1934 suburban New Jersey home. The shower divides the space in two, with the sleeping area on one side, and the bathroom on the other. Previous pages, right: The double vanity, mounted to the storage wall, floats in between the wet area and the bedroom. The sinks and the countertop are molded from a single piece of resin. Opposite: The wet area, combining the shower and the toilet, is surfaced in limestone, raised one step above the walnut-stained red-oak floors.

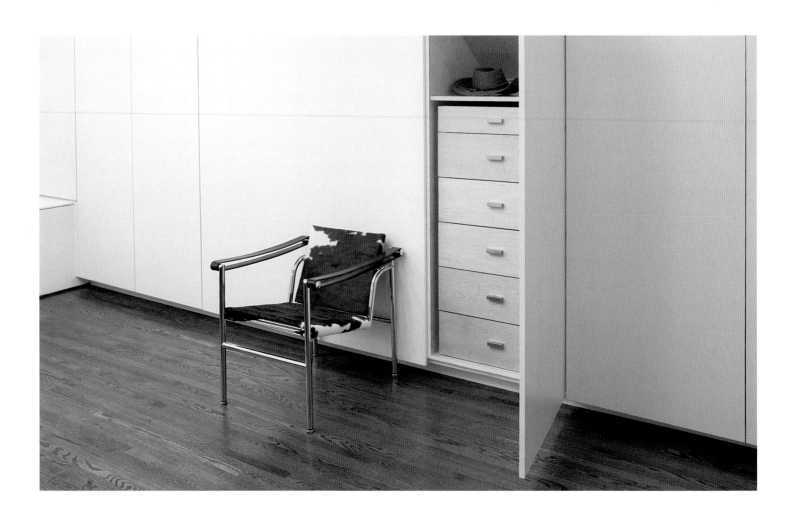

compartments extend the full length of the room, tying the sleeping and bathing spaces together. Rather than place the double vanity within the boundaries of the wet space, Dochantschi positioned it on the dividing line between the two zones, mounted to the storage wall. The sinks and countertop are molded from a single squared-off piece of smooth off-white resin that's as seamless as the segue from wet area to dry.

"To create a smooth connection between bath and bed, I turned the shower into an extended glass cube that becomes a major feature of both spaces," explains Dochantschi. "It also lets light flow from the bathroom window into the center of the room."

The shower's back wall is a beguiling expanse of heavily veined dark Emperador marble. "The spine was an opportunity to inject some texture and interest into the space; it's almost like an accent wall," says Kubany. She discovered the marble through one of her clients, architect Stefan Jaklitsch. "He had a sample sitting on his desk and I found it to be so striking and unusual. While classic, it feels very at home in this modern environment," she says.

The shift in flooring height and material from oak to limestone is the major transition point in this space with no walls. "The contrast between light and dark, between stone and wood, makes the entire wet area feel like it's floating—or gliding along like a boat," says Dochantschi. (A slim recess where the wood and stone meet adds to the effect.) The graphic quality of the architecture is reinforced by the Kubanys' choice of furnishings: bed and bath are decorated with collections of South African terra-cotta vases, mother-of-pearl inlaid Syrian antiques, and Zulu baskets woven by a female collective. "We wanted the suite to read a little European, with a hint of Africa to soften the modern lines," Kubany says.

 Despite its avant-garde look, the open-plan suite is rooted in family values. "Often when people renovate, they just build another, larger version of the kinds of rooms they already have rather than create a space that opens up a new way of living," says Dochantschi. "The master suite adds a dimension to the Kubanys' life that they didn't have before—a different kind of family togetherness than they have in other parts of the house."

Opposite, above: To maximize square footage, Dochantschi relegated storage to the otherwise unusable area under the roofline's sloping eaves. The entire wall is lined with closets and drawers, tucked behind white-stained wood doors. **Opposite, below:** The architect designed shadow gaps—or slim recesses—where two materials meet to buffer the transition of contrasting finishes. The gaps run along the bottom of every wall, and between the shower's marble spine and adjacent drywall. The shower's back wall is clad in dark Emperador marble, installed in a bricklike pattern. "I fell in love with it immediately," says Kubany. "The stone is so old world, yet so modern—especially installed in bricks instead of slabs."

resource directory

advice

American Institute of Architects (AIA)
1735 New York Avenue NW
Washington, DC 20006
800-AIA-3837
aia.org

Ceramic Tile Institute of America Inc. (CTIOA)
12061 Jefferson Boulevard
Culver City, CA 90230
310-574-7800
ctioa.org

National Association of Home Builders (NAHB)
1201 15th Street NW
Washington, DC 20005
800-368-5242
nahb.org

National Electrical Contractors Association (NECA)
NECA Connection
3 Bethesda Metro Center
Suite 1100
Bethesda, MD 20814
301-657-3110
necaconnection.com

National Kitchen & Bath Association (NKBA)
687 Willow Grove Street
Hackettstown, NJ 07840
800-843-6522
nkba.org

Plumbing Heating Cooling Contractors National Association (PHCC)
180 South Washington Street
Falls Church, VA 22046
800-533-7694
phccweb.org

architects and designers

Jeff Andrews
Jeff Andrews Design
354 West Avenue 42
Los Angeles, CA 90065
323-227-9777
jeffandrews-design.com

Peter S. Balsam
Peter S. Balsam Associates
Interior Design
1601 Third Avenue, Suite 20K
New York, NY 10128
212-831-6556
pbalsam@nyc.rr.com
peterbalsam.com

Laura Bohn
Laura Bohn Design Associates
345 Seventh Avenue, 2nd Floor
New York, NY 10001
212-645-3636
lbda.com

Barclay Butera
1745 Westcliff Drive
Newport Beach, CA 92660
949-650-8570
barclaybutera.com

Joan Chan
Joan Chan
Associate: Jose Pimentel
210 West 90th Street
New York, NY 10024
859-396-8293

Markus Dochantschi
studioMDA
102 Franklin Street, 3rd Floor
New York, NY 10013
212-343-3330
studiomda.com

Jamie Drake
Drake Design Associates
140 East 56th Street
New York, NY 10022
212-754-3099
drakedesignassociates.com

Maureen Footer
Maureen Footer Design
136 East 57th Street, Suite 503
New York, NY 10022
212-207-3400
maureenfooterdesign.com

Andy Goldsborough
41 Union Square West
Studio 1131
New York, NY 10003
212-414-1514
andygoldsborough.com

René González
670 NE 50th Terrace
Miami, FL 33137
305-762-5895
renegonzalezarchitect.com

Celerie Kemble
Kemble Interiors
224 West 30th Street
13th Floor
New York, NY 10001
212-675-9576

294 Hibiscus Avenue
Palm Beach, FL 33480
561-659-5556
kembleinteriors.com

John Loecke
John Loecke Interior Design
    & Styling Services
17 Chester Court
Brooklyn, NY 11225
917-318-0006
jloeckeinc.com

Mark Nichols
Mark Nichols Modern Interiors
1502 East Baristo Road
Palm Springs, CA 92262
760-864-1747
marknicholsinteriors.com

Benjamin Noriega-Ortiz
BNO Design
75 Spring Street, 6th Floor
New York, NY 10012
212-343-9709
bnodesign.com

Poesis Design
26 Lime Rock Road
Lakeville, CT 06039
860-435-0530
poesisdesign.com

Miles Redd
77 Bleecker Street
New York, NY 10012
212-674-0902
milesredd.com

D. Crosby Ross
310-859-7320

Scott Salvator
PO Box 20496
New York, NY 10021
212-861-5355
scottsalvator.com

Joel Sanders
Joel Sanders Architect
106 East 19th Street, 2nd Floor
New York, NY 10003
212-431-8751
joelsandersarchitect.com

Paul Siskin
Siskin Valls
21 West 58th Street
New York, NY 10019
212-752-3790

Alison Spear
Alison Spear, AIA
3815 Northeast Miami Court
Miami, FL 33137
305-438-1200
alisonspearaia.com

Stephanie Stokes
Stephanie Stokes, Inc.
139 East 57th Street
New York, NY 10022
212-756-9922
stephaniestokesinc.com

Betty Wasserman
Betty Wassterman Art &
Interiors, Ltd.
236 West 26th Street
New York, NY 10010
212-352-8476
bettywasserman.com
bettyhome.com

Workshop/APD
555 Eighth Avenue, Suite 1509
New York, NY 10018
212-273-9712
workshopapd.com

vendors

Aamsco
100 Lamp Light Circle
Summerville, SC 29483
800-221-9092

ABC Carpet & Home
888 Broadway
New York, NY 10003
212-473-3000
abchome.com

ABC Worldwide Stone Trading
234 Banker Street
Brooklyn, NY 11222
718-389-8360
abcworldwidestone.com

Accurate Glass and Mirror, Inc.
526 Route 17 South
Carlstadt, NJ 07072
866-460-1313

Adrien Linford
927 Madison Avenue
New York, NY 10021
212-628-4500

AF New York
22 West 21st Street
New York, NY 10010
212-243-5400
afnewyork.com

Aggressive Glass
346 East 92nd Street
New York, NY 10128
212-860-3333
aggressiveglass.com

Ambassador Construction Co.
317 Madison Avenue
New York, NY 10017
212-922-1020
ambassadorconstruction.com

Americh
10700 John Price Road
Charlotte, NC 28273
704-588-3075
americh.com

Amy Perlin Antiques
306 East 61st Street
New York, NY 10021
212-593-5756
amyperlinantiques.com

Ann Sacks
8935 Beverly Boulevard West
West Hollywood, CA 90048
310-273-0700
annsacks.com

Archie MacAllister
Dog Productions
917-686-4788

Artemide Lighting
1980 New Highway
Farmingdale, NY 11735
516-694-9292
artemide.com

Artistic Metal Works
925-493-1400
artisticmetalworks.net

Artistic Tile
A&D Building
150 East 58th Street
New York, NY 10155
212-838-3222
artistictile.com

Atwater Pottery
323-666-3963
atwaterpottery.com

Avonite
7350 Empire Drive
Florence, KY 41042
800-354-9858
avonitesurfaces.com

Babey Moulton Jue & Booth
510 Third Street
San Francisco, CA 94107
415-979-9880
bamo.com

Bega
bega-us.com

Benjamin Moore
benjaminmoore.com

Berbere World Imports
3049 South La Cienega
 Boulevard
Culver City, CA 90232
310-842-3842
berbereimports.com

Bernhardt Furniture
1839 Morganton Boulevard SW
Lenoir, NC 28645
828-758-9811
bernhardt.com

Bisazza
3540 NW 72nd Avenue
Miami, FL 33122
800-247-2992
bisazzausa.com

Boffi Soho
31½ Greene Street
New York, NY 10013
212-431-8282
boffi.com

The Brass Center
248 East 58th Street
New York, NY 10022
212-421-0090
thebrasscenter.com

Callaway Woodworks
11320 FM 529 Road #A
Houston, TX 77041
877-518-9698
callawaywoodworks.com

Cambridge Architectural
105 Goodwill Road
Cambridge, MD 21613
866-806-2385
cambridgearchitectural.com

Carlos de la Puente Antiques
238 East 60th Street
New York, NY 10022
212-751-4228
delapuenteantiques.com

Chris Karlson
323-377-1545

City Frames
259 West 30th Street, #5
New York, NY 10001
212-967-4401

Cjon Construction
201-488-5974

Continental Lighting
268-04 Hillside Avenue
Floral Park, NY 11001
800-560-1466
continentallightingcorp.com

Corian Products
DuPont Co.
PPD Department
Wilmington, DE 19898
800-4-CORIAN
corian.com

Counter Revolutions
973-778-5525

Czech & Speake Ltd
Through Ron Robinson
2500 South La Cienega
 Boulevard
Los Angeles, CA 90034
310-815-0606

David Duncan Antiques
247 East 60th Street
New York, NY 10022
212-688-0793
davidduncanantiques.com

Davis & Warshow
A&D Building
150 East 58th Street
New York, NY 10155
212-688-5990
daviswarshow.com

Decorators Plumbing
109 NE 39th Street
Miami, FL 33137
305-576-0022
decoratorsplumbing.com

Demolition Depot
216 East 125th Street
New York, NY 10035
212-860-1138
demolitiondepot.com

Design Bath & Hardware, Inc.
Pacific Design Center
8687 Melrose Avenue
Suite B444
Los Angeles, CA 90069
310-358-9669
designbath-hardware.com

Diamond Spas
760 South 104th Street
Broomfield, CO 80020
303-665-8303
diamondspas.com

Diva
8801 Beverly Boulevard
Los Angeles, CA 90048
310-278-3191
divafurniture.com

Donadic Woodworking, Inc.
45-25 39 Street
Long Island City, NY 11104

Donghia
979 Third Avenue, Suite 613
New York, NY 10022
212-935-3713
donghia.com

Doreen Interiors
221 West 17th Street
New York, NY 10011
212-255-9008
doreeninteriors.com

Dornbracht Americas
1700 Executive Drive South
Suite 600
Duluth, GA 30096
800-774-1181
dornbracht.com

Downtown
719 North La Cienega
   Boulevard
Los Angeles, CA 90069

Dualoy Leather
45 West 34th Street, Suite 811
New York, NY 10001
212-736-3360
dualoy.com

Duravit USA
2205 Northmont Parkway
Suite 200
Duluth, GA 30096
770-931-3575
duravit.com

Duschqueen
461 West Main Street
Wyckoff, NJ 07481
800-348-8080
duschqueenusa.com

Edelman Leather
80 Pickett District Road
New Milford, CT 06776
860-350-9600
edelmanleather.com

Emser Tile
323-650-2000
emser.com

Eurotec
84464 Cabazon Center Drive
Indio, CA 92201
760-770-4323

Farrow & Ball
8475 Melrose Avenue
Los Angeles, CA 90069
888-511-1121
farrow-ball.com

Ferguson Bath and Kitchen Gallery
8532 Melrose Avenue
West Hollywood, CA 90069
310-657-1750

Fong's Creative Construction
950 Park Avenue
New York, NY 10028
212-439-0919

Freudenberg Building Systems, Inc.
94 Glenn Street
Lawrence, MA 01843
800-332-NORA
norarubber.com

Gilly Flowers
1627 Silver Lake Boulevard
Silver Lake Village
Los Angeles, CA 90026
323-953-2910
gillyflowers.com

Glidden
1901 Ford Drive
Cleveland, OH 44106
800-454-3336
glidden.com

Gracious Home
1220 Third Avenue
New York, NY 10021
212-517-6300
gracioushome.com

Hafele America
3901 Cheyenne Drive
Archdale, NC 27263
336-434-2322
hafele.com

Hansgrohe
1490 Bluegrass Lakes Parkway
Alpharetta, GA 30004
800-488-8119
hansgrohe-usa.com

Hastings Tile
230 Park Avenue South
New York, NY 10003
212-674-9700
hastingstilebath.com

Heritage Antiques
380 East Main Street
Lexington, KY 40507
859-253-1035

Hines
Decoration and Design
   Building
979 Third Avenue
New York, NY 10022
212-754-5880

Home Depot
homedepot.com

I. Bibicoff
279 Van Brunt Street
Brooklyn, NY 11231
718-941-9100

IKEA
ikea.com

J. Edlin Interiors
150 West 26th Street
13th Floor
New York, NY 10001
212-243-2111

Jet-Line Products
80 East 26th Street
Paterson, NJ 07514
973-345-8000

John Rosselli International
523 East 73rd Street
New York, NY 10021
212-737-2252
johnrosselli.com

Julia Gray Ltd.
979 Third Avenue, Suite 711
New York, NY 10022
212-223-4454
juliagraymindwire.com

Kallista
444 Highland Drive
Kohler, WI 53044
888-4-KALLISTA
kallista.com

Kohler Co.
kohler.com

The Kohler Store
100 Merchandise Mart
Chicago, IL 60654
312-755-2510

Kosta Boda
800-351-9842
kostaboda.us

Kraft Hardware
315 East 62nd Street
New York, NY 10021
212-838-2214
krafthardware.com

Kraftworks
52 Broadway, Suite 301
New York, NY 10012
212-431-7501
kraftworksltd.com

Labrazel
1003F Farmington Avenue
West Hartford, CT 06107
860-232-6300
labrazel.com

Lefroy Brooks
850 Metropolitan Avenue
Brooklyn, NY 11211
718-302-5292
lefroybrooks.com

Lightforms
48 West 24th Street
New York, NY 10011
212-255-4664
lightformsinc.com

Lighting Collaborative Inc.
333 Park Avenue South
Suite 2B
New York, NY 10010
212-253-7220
lightingcollaborative.com

Linea
8843-49 Beverly Boulevard
Los Angeles, CA 90048
310-273-5425
linea-inc.com

Liz's Antique Hardware
453 South La Brea
Los Angeles, CA 90036
323-939-4403
lahardware.com

Luminaire
4040 NE Second Avenue
Miami, FL 33137
305-576-5788
luminaire.com

Lutron
7200 Suter Road
Coopersburg, PA 18036
610-282-3800
lutron.com

Melinda Stickney Gibson
PO Box 461
Phoenicia, NY 12464
845-688-2053
mstickneygibson@aol.com

Miami Stone District
335 NE 59th Terrace
Miami, FL 33137
305-762-7930

Michaela Scherrer Interior Design
536 Rosemont Avenue
Pasadena, CA 91103
michaelascherrer.com

Mike Pell
212-582-7099

Modern Arc
1014 Pico Boulevard
Santa Monica, CA 90405
310-255-0982
modernarcinc.com

Mrs. MacDougall, Inc.
Through Hinson & Company
979 Third Avenue
Suite 732
New York, NY 10022
212-688-5538

Munimula
548 Squires Road
Quincy, MI 49082
517-605-5343
munimula.com

Neo-Metro
15125 Proctor Avenue
City of Industry, CA 91746
800-591-9050
neo-metro.com

Nicholas Antiques
979 Third Avenue
New York, NY 10022
212-688-3312
nicholasantiques.com

O&C Builders
104 Crandon Boulevard, #315
Key Biscayne, FL 33149
305-361-1125
ocbuilders.com

Olde Good Things
1800 South Grand Avenue
Los Angeles, CA 90015
213-746-8600
oldegoodthings.com

145 Antiques
27 West 20th Street
New York, NY 10011
212-807-1149
145antiques.com

Osborne & Little
979 Third Avenue
Suite 520
New York, NY 10022
212-751-3333

Paris Ceramics
150 East 58th Street, 7th Floor
New York, NY 10155
212-644-2782
parisceramics.com

Patterson Flynn & Martin
979 Third Avenue, Suite 632
New York, NY 10022
212-688-7700

Paul Stamati Gallery
1050 Second Avenue
New York, NY 10022
212-754-4533
stamati.com

Pottery Barn Kids
800-993-4923
potterybarnkids.com

R. B. Wyatt Manufacturing Co.
PO Box 404 Ryder Station
Brooklyn, NY 11234
718-209-9682
rbwyattshowerdoor.com

Red Hook Marble
31 Coffey Street
Brooklyn, NY 11231
718-625-5291
redhookmarble.com

Restoration Hardware
800-910-9836
restorationhardware.com

Runtal
187 Neck Road
Ward Hill, MA 01835
800-526-2621
runtalnorthamerica.com

Sherle Wagner, LLC
300 East 62nd Street
New York, NY 10065
212-758-3300
sherlewagner.com

Short Hills Marble and Tile
658 Morris Turnpike
Short Hills, NJ 07078
973-376-1330

Simons Hardware and Bath
421 Third Avenue
New York, NY 10016
212-532-9220
simons-hardware.com

Specialty Hardware & Plumbing
283 South Robertson
   Boulevard
Beverly Hills, CA 90211
310-659-9351
specialtyhardware.net

Spirit of Wood
011-887-829-899
spirit-of-wood.com

Square Deal Plumbing and Supplies
2302 East Florence Avenue
Huntington Park, CA 90255
323-587-8291

Stephen E. Balser
Art-In-Construction Ltd.
55 Washington Street, #653
Brooklyn, NY 11201
718-222-3874

Steven Amedee Framing
41 North Moore Street
New York, NY 10013
212-343-1696

Stone Source
215 Park Avenue South
New York, NY 10003
212-979-6400
stonesource.com

Taighean Builders
860-738-0843

Takashimaya
693 Fifth Avenue
New York, NY 10022
212-350-0100
ny-takashimaya.com

Telmont Construction
306 East 11th Street, 4A
New York, NY 10003
917-304-0561

Terzano Cabinetry
25 Ruta Court
South Hackensack, NJ 07606
201-373-9500
terzanocabinetry.com

3-D Construction
175 West Broadway
New York, NY 10013
212-219-2120

3-Form
2300 South 2300 West, Suite B
Salt Lake City, UT 84119
800-726-0126
3-form.com

Topdeq
3 Security Drive, Suite 303
Cranbury, NJ 08512
866-876-3300
topdeq.com

Toto USA
25 Mercer Street
New York, NY 10013
888-295-8134
totousa.com

Urban Archeology
143 Franklin Street
New York, NY 10013
212-431-4646
urbanarcheology.com

Valtekz
2125 Southend Drive
Suite 251
Charlotte, NC 28203
704-332-5277
valtekz.com

Victoria Hagan
654 Madison Avenue
New York, NY 10065
212-888-3241
victoriahagan.com

Villeroy & Boch
5 Vaughn Drive, Suite 303
Princeton, NJ 08540
609-734-7800
villeroy-boch.com

Vitra
29 Ninth Avenue
New York, NY 10014
212-463-5700
vitra.com

Vitraform
3500 Blake Street
Denver, CO 80205
888-338-5725
vitraform.com

Vola
Through Hastings Tile and Bath
150 East 58th Street
New York, NY 10155
800-351-0038

Wainlands
800-843-9237
wainlands.com

Walker Zanger
8750 Melrose Avenue
West Hollywood, CA 90069
310-659-1234
walkerzanger.com

Ward Architectural
900 Broadway, Suite 204
New York, NY 10003
212-979-5363
wardarchitectural.com

Waterworks
23 West Putnam Avenue
Greenwich, CT 06830
203-869-7766
waterworks.com

Wetstyle
276 Saint-Jacques
Montréal, QC
Canada, H2Y 1N3
866-842-1367
wetstyle.net

Wholesale Marble Fabrication
150 East 58th Street
New York, NY 10155
212-223-4068
wholesalemarbleandgranite.com

Zale Contracting Inc.
1740 Decatur Street
Ridgewood, NY 11385
718-366-1092

Zelen
8055 Beverly Boulevard
Los Angeles, CA 90048
323-658-6756
zelenhome.com

Zumtobel Lighting Inc.
3300 Route 9W
Highland, NY 12528
800-448-4131
zumtobelstaff.com

materials and sources

escapes

Bathing au Naturel 19
DESIGNER: MICHAELA SCHERRER
Vanity cabinetry: to the trade by Chris Karlson; vanity sinks: Jay Aaron Stone through Specialty Hardware & Plumbing; sink faucets and fixtures: Antonio Lupi through Modern Arc; cabinet hardware: Michaela Scherrer Interior Design; teak shower grid: custom to the trade by Chris Karlson; vanity lighting, floor pouf: Michaela Scherrer Interior Design; tub faucet and fixtures, showerhead fixtures: Specialty Hardware & Plumbing; palm leaf: Gilly Flowers; tub faucet and fixtures, showerhead: Antonio Lupi through Modern Arc.

Yachtsman's Haven 26
DESIGNER: SCOTT SALVATOR
Flooring: Paris Ceramics; vanity cabinetry, wall panels: Donadic Woodworking, Inc.; vanity lighting, mirror, sink, cabinet hardware: Sherle Wagner, LLC; faucet, fixtures, showerhead, towel rack: Czech & Speake Ltd; glass wall dividers: R. B. Wyatt Manufacturing Co.; toilet: Waterworks; lighting above toilet: Mrs. MacDougall, Inc.; shower tile: Paris Ceramics.

A Modern Approach to Zen Style 29
DESIGNER: JEFF ANDREWS
Floor tile: Isreali Blue–AS2362-1, Ann Sacks; wall tile: Selumggio/Grigio, Ann Sacks; shower tile: Limestone–Flannel, Walker Zanger; shower bench tile: black honed granite, Emser Tile; vanity sink, faucets, fixtures, mirror, showerhead: Ann Sacks; vanity countertop: Pompignan/AS7833-2, Ann Sacks; vanity cabinets: custom by Jeff Andrews Design; tub: Happy D, Duravit through Ferguson Bath and Kitchen Gallery; tub tile: Limestone–Flannel, Walker Zanger; tub faucet: Ann Sacks; lighting pendant: vintage from Downtown; toilet: Duravit through Ferguson Bath and Kitchen Gallery; chair: Berbere Imports; pottery: Atwater Pottery by Adam Silverman.

Set in Stone 36
ARCHITECT: RENÉ GONZÁLEZ
Flooring, vanity, wall marble: Miami Stone District; tub, vanity sink: Agape at Luminaire; vanity mirror: custom by O&C Builders; sink faucets, tub faucet, fixtures: Vola through Decorators Plumbing; stool: E15 at Luminaire; toilet, urinal: Duravit through Decorators Plumbing.

A Star Turn 39
ARCHITECT: D. CROSBY ROSS
Wall tile: translucent aqua glass, Walker Zanger; floor tile: Metallismo stainless steel, Walker Zanger; showerhead: Ann Sacks through Lefroy Brooks; vanity/sink (Axolo X Fly sink in wengé wood and crystal, Model #XFLC1) and vanity mirror (Simplice from Maxalto), Diva, custom design by D. Crosby Ross; toilet: Neo-Metro Collection, Metro-Urban toilet at Design Bath & Hardware, Inc.; urinal: Neo-Metro Collection, Contour urinal at Design Bath & Hardware, Inc.; tub: Japanese soaking tub by architect-designer Jim Olson for Diamond Spas; chair: Verner Panton S Chair, Vitra; side cabinet: Pandora Silver, Linea; outdoor showerhead: Ann Sacks.

Rhapsody in Blues 47
DESIGNER: BARCLAY BUTERA
Please go to BarclayButera.com for material and source information.

small spaces

Hide and Seek 59
ARCHITECTS: MATTHEW BERMAN AND ANDREW KOTCHEN OF WORKSHOP/APD
Toilet: stainless steel, Neo-Metro; tile: 4 x 4 antique brown tile, Edelman Leather; faucet, accessories: XO by Lefroy Brooks; wall art: custom-designed by Workshop/APD.

Blue Crush 64
DESIGNER: JAMIE DRAKE
Flooring: Stone Source; wall paint: Venetian plaster, Benjamin Moore's 2055-30, Caribbean Blue Water; shower curtain fabric: Osborne & Little; side chair: Victoria Hagan; wastebasket: Labrazel; toilet: Toto.

Cargo Space 71
DESIGNER: STEPHANIE STOKES
Construction: 3-D Construction; lighting: Mike Pell; faucet, fixtures: Dornbracht through Gracious Home; sinks: Kohler.

Museum Quality 77
DESIGNER: MAUREEN WILSON FOOTER
Vanity legs, basin, faucet, door hardware: Sherle Wagner, LLC; toilet: Waterworks.

entertaining

Having It Both Ways 87
ARCHITECTS: ROB BRISTOW AND PILAR PROFFITT OF POESIS DESIGN
Master Bath
Cabinetry, vanity mirror, shelves: custom by Poesis Design; cabinet hardware: Hafele; vanity lighting: Artemide Lighting; sinks, toilet, tub: Duravit through Hafele; faucets, fixtures, showerhead: Dornbracht; windows: custom by Taighean Builders.
Spa
Flooring: custom by Taighean Builders; vanity mirror, wood shelf, shower: custom by Poesis Design; vanity lighting: Artemide Lighting; spa/sauna, bucket: Callaway Woodworks; bidet, toilet: Duravit; faucets, fixtures: Dornbracht; door pulls: Hafele.

Shine On 96
DESIGNER: MILES REDD
Chairs: antique French, Amy Perlin Antiques; Chinese garden stools, John Rosselli International.

Raising the Bar 99
DESIGNER: BENJAMIN NORIEGA-ORTIZ
Toilet, towel rack, shower door, shower lights, shower fixtures, shower tile, rug, stool, fan, chair, fabric treatment, mirrored console, recessed lighting, sink faucet, sink lavatory, flooring: custom by Benjamin Noriega-Ortiz.

Entertainment Value 107
DESIGNERS: JOHN LOECKE AND JASON OLIVER NIXON
Tile: penny round, Ann Sacks; sink, sconces, vanity: Barbara Barry for Kallista; toilet, shower, water tiles: Kohler; cabinet: vintage Dorothy Draper from ebay.com; lighting components: Radio RA by Lutron; mirror: Martha Stewart Signature for Bernhardt Furniture; floor paint: Farrow & Ball; wall paint: Glidden.

His, Hers, and Theirs 115
DESIGNER: PAUL SISKIN
Fixtures, faucets, tub, accessories: Waterworks; tile: stone and mosaic, Artistic Tile; chairs: ABC Carpet & Home; carpets: Patterson Flynn & Martin.

modern boudoirs

A Stone's Throw from Pompeii 127
DESIGNER: PETER S. BALSAM
Flooring: Artistic Tile; lighting, shower fixtures, bath faucet: Sherle Wagner, LLC; marble: ABC Worldwide Stone Trading; cabinets: Zale Contracting Inc.; shower door: I. Bibicoff; tub: Kohler through Davis & Warshow; tub pendant: Mrs. MacDougall.

Bathing Beauty 133
DESIGNER: CELERIE KEMBLE
Cabinet: antique French apothecary table (circa 1910) from 145 Antiques, converted to a closet by Archie McAllister, constructed by Telmont Construction; blue faux-leather inside closets: Celerie Kemble for Valtekz; chair: 1stdibs.com; slipcover: constructed by J. Edlin Interiors out of Restoration Hardware towels; lights, sconces: Restoration Hardware; wallpaper: Farrow & Ball; flooring: Carrara basket weave, Cardoglio dot, Urban Archeology; walls: Carrara marble, Nemo tile, Urban Archeology; tub: antique from Demolition Depot; sink, tub fixtures: nickel Etoile line, Waterworks; basins: hammered nickel, Waterworks; sink top: custom by Kemble Interiors for Red Hook Marble; sink legs: Urban Archeology; mirrors: custom by City Frames; vintage buttons and charcoal drawing frames: Steven Amedee Framing; knobs, shower door: Kraft Hardware; towels: Waterworks; fake succulents in wicker: Adrien Linford.

Age of Opulence 139
DESIGNERS: PAMELA BABEY AND ALAN DEAL OF BABEY MOULTON JUE & BOOTH
General contractor and electrical: John Chiusolo and Craig Stelakis of Cjon Construction; mosaic: Calacatta Gold floor design with water-jet inset in sable onyx, Nancy Epstein for Artistic Tile; chandeliers: René Lalique, Paul Stamati Gallery; marble door frames, arches, marble walls: Breccia Imperiale, Artistic Tile; metalwork, ceiling detail, shelf and vanity frames: Julius Miniverni for Artistic Metal Works; shower tile: Artistic Tile Opera Glass Silato pattern, Nancy Epstein for Artistic Tile; cabinetry, shagreen application, vanity assembly: Joe Terzano for Terzano Cabinetry; vanity tops: Breccia Imperiale marble stone slabs from Artistic Tile fabricated by Ralph Baione for Wholesale Marble Fabrication; backsplash, stone slabs: Breccia Imperiale marble from Artistic Tile fabricated by Lenny Ventigmilia for Counter Revolutions; bath hardware: Dornbracht Obina through Artistic Tile; hand-etched glass sinks: Vitraform through Artistic Tile; Stucco Venezia: Peter Lyons for Kraftworks; steam-shower door: Duschqueen; in-floor fiber-optic night lighting: Fiberstars through Jet-Line Products; glass ball sconces above sinks: custom-made in France through Babey Moulton Jue & Booth; toilet: Toto washlet through Artistic Tile; ceiling glazing: 3-Form; shagreen: Dualoy Leather; door frames: Blacklip seashell inlay custom through Artistic Tile.

Light and Lively 147
DESIGNER: JOAN CHAN
Antique pendant, sconces: Carlos de la Puente Antiques; antique chandelier (dressing room): David Duncan Antiques; dressing door, dresser knobs: The Brass Center; hardware, plumbing trims: Sherle Wagner, LLC; contractor: Ambassador Construction Co.; custom cabinetry: Fong's Creative Construction; flowers: Takashimaya; etched doors: Heritage Antiques.

voyeur

A Postmodern Prewar 157
ARCHITECT: JOEL SANDERS
DESIGNER: ANDY GOLDSBOROUGH
Vanity mirrors: Aggressive Glass; vanity light fixtures: Wever Ducre through Lighting Collaborative Inc.; countertop, sink: Corian Glacier White, DuPont; shower curtain: Glant frosted sheer through Hines; sink faucet and fixtures: Dornbracht Tara Classic wall mount through AF New York; towel rack: Boffi Soho; shower door: acid-etched blue glass, Aggressive Glass; shower fixtures: Lefroy Brooks through Simons Hardware and Bath.

Making a Splash 165
DESIGNER: MARK NICHOLS
Vanity cabinetry: Eurotec; wall tile, glass tile: Walker Zanger; tub: Codex through Ann Sacks; sink: Loop, Villeroy & Boch; vanity mirror: Aamsco; dresser, side cabinet: Eurotec.

Peekaboo, I See You 173
ARCHITECT: ALISON SPEAR
Countertops: Corian, DuPont; cabinetry, mirrors: Spirit of Wood; bathtub: Happy D, Duravit; tile: Bisazza; light fixtures: Luminaire.

The Greenhouse Effect 179
DESIGNER: LAURA BOHN
Flooring: Hastings Tile; vanity mirrors: Restoration Hardware; vanity light fixtures: Lightforms; vanity: Munimula; sink fixtures: AF New York; sink: Wet, Wetstyle; room divider: Topdeq; backsplash tile: Avonite; sinks, faucets, fixtures: Vola through Hastings Tile; shower tile: Waterworks; shower fixtures: Philippe Starck for Hansgrohe; shower lights: Artemide Lighting; tub: Americh; tub tile: Ward Architectural; toilet: Toto; chair: Donghia.

Room and Board 184
ARCHITECT: RENÉ GONZÁLEZ
Please go to ReneGonzalezArchitect.com for material and source information.

family baths

A Family Affair 191
DESIGNER: MICHAELA SCHERRER
Mom's Bathroom
Vanity countertop, open shelf: custom by Michaela Scherrer vintage collection; vanity mirror: Zelen; standing tub fixture, stool: custom by Michaela Scherrer; small side chair: Olde Good Things; jewelry holder: Zelen.
Younger Boys' Bathroom
Flooring: Nora Rubber through Freudenberg Building Systems, Inc.; sink lavatory: restored schoolhouse sink through Square Deal Plumbing and Supplies; sink faucet: old/new stock Chicago through Square Deal Plumbing and Supplies; vanity mirror: IKEA; vanity lights: Liz's Antique Hardware; toilet: Square Deal Plumbing and Supplies; shower: Michaela Scherrer vintage collection through Michaela Scherrer Interior Design; corrugated tin: Home Depot.
Oldest Boy's Bathroom
Wash basin, faucet, fixtures: Square Deal Plumbing and Supplies; flooring: Nora Rubber through Freudenberg Building Systems, Inc.; mirrors: IKEA.

Storybook Bath 198
DESIGNER: PETER S. BALSAM
Tile: Artistic Tile; lavatory sink, toilet: Kohler through Davis & Warshow; shower, tub fixtures: Grohe through Davis & Warshow; cabinets: Zale Contracting Inc.; vanity mirror: Julia Gray Ltd.; sink and tub: Waterworks; overhead light: Nicholas Antiques; hardware and pulls: Kraft Hardware.

Bubble Bath at the Beach 201
DESIGNER: BETTY WASSERMAN
Vanity, vanity mirror: custom by Betty Wasserman Art & Interiors, Ltd.; faucet, fixtures, sink: Waterworks; toilet: Toto; wall tile: subway tiles from Stone Source; showerhead, fixtures: Waterworks; artwork: Melinda Stickney Gibson; rug: Pottery Barn Kids; shutters: Doreen Interiors.

All Together Now 209
ARCHITECT: MARKUS DOCHANTSCHI OF STUDIOMDA
Floor tiles: French Vanilla Limestone by Short Hills Marble and Tile; lavatory sink: wet VC60 through AF New York; sink faucet: MEM series, Dornbracht through AF New York; vanity lighting: Modular International through Continental Lighting; vanity mirror: Robern at AF New York; shower fixtures: MEM series, Dornbracht through AF New York; shower door/walls: Accurate Glass and Mirror, Inc.; shower tiles: Dark Emperador Marble by Short Hills Marble and Tile; showerhead: Axor, Hansgrohe through AF New York; overhead light: Modular International through Continental Lighting; door handle: Sugatsune through Simon's Hardware and Bath; toilet: Philippe Starck for Duravit through AF New York.

acknowledgments

This book would not have been possible without the support and generosity of many people. I am grateful to my collaborators: Jen Renzi, coproducer and writer, and photographer Andrew French. I'm indebted to Doris Cooper, editorial director at Clarkson Potter, who discovered me, befriended me, and was a delight to work with.

I'd also like to thank Clarkson Potter publisher Lauren Shakely, who championed the book from day one, and Jane Treuhaft, Sibylle Kazeroid, Aliza Fogelson, Lindsay Miller, and Kim Tyner at Potter. Callie Jenschke also merits thanks for her thorough research. Richard Ferretti deserves special recognition for lending his exceptional design talents to *The Luxury Bathroom*.

I'd be remiss if I did not acknowledge the designers, architects, and their clients who provided the projects featured in this book. Their genius is *The Luxury Bathroom*.

Thanks also go to my colleagues at *Met Home*—Donna Warner, Deborah Burns, and Christine Boyle—for their wise counsel and endless encouragement.

I deeply appreciate the great professional advice from design-industry gurus Esther Perman, Janice Langrall, and Valerie Moran. I'd also like to thank Jim and Nancy Druckman who, nearly a decade ago, gave me my first job in the design industry.

On a personal note, I want to thank Elaine Griffin and Rebecca Dreyfus, who counseled and calmed me during this project. I am also indebted to my friends and cheerleaders: Kirsten Brant, Christopher Coleman, Patrick Danek, Diana Friedman, Lisa Garber, Bonnie Lasek, Jill Levine, Heather Maloney, Joanne Maurno, Karen Rowe, Natasha Ruiz-Gomez, Scott Salvator, and Doug Wilson. Thank you for making me laugh during the chaotic months while I moved, changed jobs, had a baby, and completed my first book. My sister, Jackie Jewett, and her amazing family gave me strength when I felt like giving up—if she and her husband could raise six kids, then I could finish *The Luxury Bathroom*. I am also grateful to my mother and father, Bobbi and Larry Wayne, whose blind faith now appears fruitful.

And, finally, I'd like to thank my husband, Michael, whose patience, understanding, proofreading, and computer savvy fostered *The Luxury Bathroom*'s completion.

index